VATICAN II

*This volume is dedicated to
the memory of
Bishop Charles R. Mulrooney,
one of the Council fathers
who taught me the meaning
of true Christian Humanism*

Contents

Preface

It was an unforgettable day. The river of white miters flowed out the bronze doors, through the colonnade and across the square, finally ascending the rise to enter the largest church in Christendom. Well over two thousand — the largest assembly of bishops the world had ever seen. And then came the old man who had ended up on top of the heap, as he put it. The Vicar of Christ on earth, who knew who he was and dared to call upon the Father to send forth the Spirit in a new Pentecost. This day, October 12, 1962, gave visible form to that outpouring. In less than a year the "old man" would have himself gone to the Father, but the outpouring would go on. It was only a beginning. And most of us that day hadn't a clue as to what was really beginning to unfold.

The vast majority of those I was with were products of the old seminary training. We had studied our theology in manuals where thesis after thesis was proved, giving us an illusionary assurance that we had it all wrapped up. Scripture texts were marshalled to prove the point and then documents of the Church. Primary among them were the texts from the ecumenical councils, those most special moments in the life of the Church when it spoke most absolutely: *anathema sit,*

let him be damned, who dared to disagree. And now we were
standing in a council!

Most of the American bishops, and I suspect very many
of those from other nations, expected this to be a largely
ceremonial event. Preparatory commissions had worked long
and hard on the many texts that had been sent out. These
were to be discussed — but there seemed little enough to dis-
cuss. It was all there as we had learned it in the seminary.
There would be some votes, a signing, a solemn promulgation. And then the bishops would return to their everyday
task of guiding their flocks back home. In the first sessions
commissions of Council fathers were duly proposed. They
were to examine the texts prior to discussion. These lists
of proposed candidates were also carefully prepared by the
same ones who so carefully prepared the texts. All had been
programmed. And then...

A true Council father, Cardinal Lienart of Lille, rose from
his seat on the fourth morning and took the microphone.
There was no doubt in his mind who was the Council that
was endowed with the special divine guidance our divine
Founder promised to his Church. It was not the preparatory
commissions. It was the fathers assembled. And it was for the
fathers assembled to decide who would be the commissioners
to examine the texts and prepare them for debate.

It was a moment of incarnation. A council was no longer
something that descended whole from the heavens. It was
a group of men from every tribe and nation gathered together in a basilica, listening to what the Spirit had to say
to the churches today. It was men of great learning and little learning, the practical pastors, the ivory-tower thinkers,
the idealists and pragmatists, the forward looking and those
who fearfully clung to the past; men who had very different ideas about what it meant to be truly conservative,
truly traditional; men who had very different ideas about

the development of doctrine or the possibility of such a thing.

Yes, it was *men*. It would be literally years before a woman was welcomed into this assembly, and then only as a guest. And the fathers had very different ideas about that, too. It was a beginning, an exciting beginning that grew in excitement as it went on. There were dull, tiresome days. Interventions that hardly revealed the breathing of the Spirit. Long, hard-working commission sessions. Late-night study. Off-the-cuff compromise and tough politicking. The Church like its Founder is incarnate and never was it so incarnated as when these two thousand plus successors of the apostles worked together through four years in all sorts of situations, seeking to honestly discern, in both a truly supernatural and in a truly human way, what the Spirit was saying to the Church and to the world in 1962, 1963, 1964, and 1965.

M. BASIL PENNINGTON

Our Lady of Joy Monastery
Lantau, China
Feast of St. Joseph, Patron of
*   the Universal Church, 1994*

Introduction

Vatican II — Dead or Alive?

"Vatican II — it's dead!" That was the flat-out answer of one of my confreres. I have been asking this question of many (and of myself): What does Vatican II mean to you today? From most the response has been relatively negative. Many, like the friend mentioned, had lived with the growing hopes of the 1930s and 1940s as currents of what was going on in France and Germany quietly flowed into the American scene. Then there was the tremendous enthusiasm of the 1960s, the demoralizing disillusionment of the 1970s, and the deadness of the 1980s. As one who had been with me in college put it: there was a great openness — and then the iron gates closed again.

Not every one sees it this way. Some see the 1960s as a time of chaos. An old man opened not only windows but doors and everything else and let in every conceivable idea and then some. His feeble successor rather unsuccessfully tried to corral some of the madness and bring it under control. It has been only in these recent years that a strong hand from Poland has begun to reestablish some true order. There

I

is a long way to go — the damage has been beyond anyone's greatest fears — but now there is some hope.

On reflection though, most — not all — concede or celebrate the fuller role Scripture plays in our lives, the liturgical renewal, the universal call to holiness, the growth in a true catholicity as many cultures and ethnic groups find their place among the People of God.

I must admit there are some nostalgic cords struck in my own soul when I attend Mass in China. But the skimpy fiddle-back vestments, beautifully embroidered though they be, and the mumbled, wholly unintelligible Latin (even to one who speaks Latin fluently) of a celebrant who has his back to us, along with the popular devotions to which the congregation is loudly giving expression, do not invite me to be deeply one with Christ's priestly prayer.

For most Catholics it was in the celebration of the liturgy that they first and most immediately experienced the renewal. However, liturgical developments are not the only fruit of Vatican II that has been widely experienced. There has been a significant emancipation of thought. I realize that "emancipation" is a loaded word; it usually connotes — at least in America — a release from slavery. Some would say that that is not an inaccurate connotation here. Others would rather liken our former state to that of children. We had learned our catechism well. We made few distinctions. We lived what we had been taught or felt guilty when we departed from it. Any other course was tantamount to leaving the Church and indeed usually expressed itself in that way. We didn't seem to realize that a certain amount of freedom and personal responsibility are necessary if one is going to live a mature faith. *Fides quaerens intellectum.* Quite rightly, faith seeks understanding. It needs to be an informed faith. It needs to know what truly is of faith, what the Church actually teaches and with what degree of certitude. In a country like America very many Catholics have been blessed with a good education, at least through high school and often through college and on to advanced degrees. Their secular learning has been quite extensive. And yet for many of these same persons religious education ended with First Communion or Confirmation or an hour a week in high school. A child's faith — childish, not childlike — is vying with a much more powerfully developed secularity.

The problem is compounded by the vagueness of the parameters of the ordinary magisterium. We have just seen Galileo rightly exonerated. It took a cautious and defensive Roman magisterium centuries to do it. A serious Catholic of today, rightly disposed though he or she may be, might well ask if the present Church teachers are not just as benighted in the area of sexuality and some other areas. These teachers seem to have remained immovable since Pius XII's memorable talk to midwives, which quietly addressed his predecessor's strictures against rhythm, the rhythm now so strongly promoted. Such questioning on the part of the faithful frequently leads to a complete dismissal of the Church's competence to guide even in areas where guidance is greatly needed. Who determines the parameters for a *fides quaerens,* a seeking faith. What is true freedom in the area of faith? We will look at Vatican II's very significant Declaration concerning Religious Freedom. We will also find in the Constitution concerning Church and the Pastoral Constitution concerning Church in the Modern World important attitudes to guide us as we face the diversity of our responses and seek to live them out.

Recently Archbishop Hayes, the retired archbishop of Halifax, referred to himself as belonging to "an endangered species," one of the 2,500 "infallibles" who signed the documents on December 7, 1965. I would say: Not an endangered species but one that is done for (just as is the species to which the author belongs, the *periti*). For better or worse, this particular species is destined to extinction. For four fall semesters these men gathered from all the corners of the earth and sat in the school of not only an amazing array of masters — theological, scriptural, canonical, and liturgical — but also in the school of Holy Spirit. What kind of marks they got we will know only on judgment day, but one has more than a little reason to think that they will not have straight As. Certainly, they were guided by the Spirit, and when they spoke as a college along with their head, they were infallibly preserved from saying anything erroneous. They certainly did not pretend to say all there is to be said on any given subject. Yet one wonders how much of what they did say corporately the individual bishops actually grasped and incorporated effectively into the living faith that has guided them in the succeeding years "back home." Many bishops, even those who faithfully attended every session, will with a humble honesty admit that there is much more in the documents than they have been able to fully comprehend and effectively live.

To my experience most of the bishops were eager students during those four fall sessions. They listened to the large coterie of surrounding *periti*. (The Latin word means "experts," though most of the men who bore that title at the Council would be quick to disclaim their expertise. In face of the matter we were working with — the wisdom of God imparted to us humans by the Son of God — everyone is a rank novice.) They pondered and prayed, discussed and questioned, and listened again with a critical ear. They certainly grew as the days of "class" unfolded. And they learned many things quickly enough.

In seminary days we had all heard so often: "Trent said...", "the Vatican Council condemned...", the Fourth Lateran defined...." The ecumenical councils seemed like numinous oracles that descended straight from heaven. There was an aura about them. When we came to Rome in October 1962, most of us were not ready for the incarnation. Many bishops — the Americans not the least among them — arrived expecting little more than ceremonies, reading of prepared documents and solemn affirmations and signings. It would be a short enough affair, albeit most solemn — and it might make a difference. For many of these bishops the breakthrough moment came in the first working session of the Council when one of the fathers stood up and claimed the Council for them, demanding that they, the bishops assembled, choose their own committees and write their own documents rather than rubber-stamp the work of the pre-conciliar Roman commissions. As the various national groups of bishops met in caucus to choose their candidates for the various commissions, they began to take possession of the Council, to experience it as theirs, under Holy Spirit. Soon enough the political maneuvering that belongs to any incarnational group was fully at play. The challenge now was to keep strong the faith that Holy Spirit was working through all of this in the unique way that the Spirit has always worked in and through an ecumenical council.

Interpret the Second Vatican Council as you may — and the interpretations I have heard have surely covered the whole conceivable spectrum — we are living in what is called and is a post-conciliar period. The Council is not over until it is over. We tend to forget that an important part of any council, if not *the* important part, is the reception of that council and its teaching by the People of God. Historically this phase of the ecumenical councils has been very diverse. The union of the Byzantine and Roman Churches at the Council of Florence in fact was never received. In some cases the reception of a council's teaching and decrees took literally centuries. The marriage legislation of the Council of Trent, whose sessions ended in the sixteenth century, went into effect or was effectively received in the United States only in 1912! The enormous shift in perspective, if not in direction, Holy Spirit has asked of the People of God through the Second Vatican Council is not going to take place overnight, nor in the course of many nights. The three decades we have lived through are little more than a long weekend in the centuries-long history of the Church. Changes have come — and changes have gone — but the real reception of Vatican II has hardly begun.

Change is always difficult. And it gets more difficult as one gets older. And the Church was beginning to get old. In many areas there had been little change since the defensive Council of Trent. In the early days of our century the Church waged an intense campaign against "modernism." Secularity was decried. Science was in fact much feared, even if some faint-hearted overtures were made in its direction. Humanism, too, was generally seen as dangerous even though we sometimes touted a Christian humanism and pointed to such martyrs as St. Thomas More. Rather than change, we proudly pointed to our lack of change. Not a word had been changed in the Eucharistic prayer of the Roman Mass since the fourth century — or so it was said. Indeed, it was actually taught that it would be a mortal sin for any priest to deliberately change any single word of that age-old prayer. What a shiver went down the backs of many when an old pontiff, who was historically more knowledgeable than most, introduced the name of Joseph into the prayer. Change is here — rapid, unceasing change. And it is here to stay, as the Council fathers themselves very emphatically acknowledged.

What now, as we live our way through the 1990s and on into a new millennium; what are we to expect?

It is a special and demanding grace to live in a post-conciliar period. There have been only twenty such gatherings in the course of the long history of the Church.

And never before one of such magnitude as this, with such breadth of vision. It was not convoked to respond to the challenge of some particular heresy or even some large-scale eruption in the Church. It was called to enliven the whole of the human family with the challenge of the fullness of what it means to be a human person and the challenge of the fullness of the teachings of Jesus Christ and what these can mean in our times.

The great synod published in fact sixteen documents: four constitutions, nine decrees, and three declarations, as well as some short messages. The four constitutions are the more important, not in name only but in fact. The Council fathers began their work with its Constitution concerning the Sacred Liturgy: *Sacrosanctum Concilium.* It was the place to begin. When the Council opened, the liturgical movement in the Church was very much alive and had been for some decades, especially in France and Germany, though also in the United States and other countries. Theologians and liturgists had produced many fine studies. And there were not only ideas on paper, there was also a good bit of practical experience. Out of this wealth an exceptionally fine pre-conciliar commission crafted one of the best schemata to be brought to the Council, indeed the only significant product of the pre-conciliar commissions to substantially survive the serious study of the fathers. Besides this excellent preparation and the readiness of the matter for consideration, there is the fact that it is here in the liturgy that the Church most truly lives, here we reach the summit of our activity as Church, one with our Head. Here the renewal can most immediately and practically touch the lives of all of the faithful. The liturgical life of the Church would reflect and make effectively present the deeper theological and spiritual renewal: *lex orandi, lex credendi.* The way we pray is the way we believe. The way we believe will express itself in the way we pray. Our renewed faith and our renewed faith community needed the space and the vehicle to express our renewed life.

But we need a deep understanding of ourselves in order to be able to express ourselves in a way that is not only adequate and satisfying but contributes to ongoing growth. So it was not only to complete the unfinished work of the First Vatican Council but to equip ourselves to move forward that the Council addressed itself to who we are as Church and most specifically as to who the Council fathers themselves are as the college of bishops, the successors of the college of apostles chosen by the Lord to shepherd his Church. It is only when we are willing to be fully who we are that we can be to the whole human family and its growth and development all that we are supposed to be as Church, as Christ in the world today.

To do this we need to be open to and in touch with our source as fully as possible. The liturgy can provide the time and place for us to practically exercise and experience this as community. But we also need to do this in a professional way, employing all the tools and resources modern developments make available to us. The Council therefore turned its attention to this and produced a clear and concise statement and directives in the Dogmatic Constitution concerning Divine Revelation (*Dei verbum*).

The Dogmatic Constitution concerning Church (*Lumen gentium*) is the pivotal document of Vatican II. This is the Church that flows forth from the source of the divine Revelation. It is the Church who prays in the liturgy. And it is the Church that must be at the heart of the world if it is to fulfill the vision not only of the saintly pontiff who convoked the Council but of the Divine Founder of the Church. The Pastoral Constitution concerning Church in the Modern World is the blueprint for the fulfillment of the vision of the Council. It is the constitution that most truly expresses the Council, that is a product of the Council. It in no way comes from the pre-conciliar commissions. It came forth from the heart of the Council as the fathers entered into their work and attuned themselves to the guiding Spirit. The constitution's popular Latin name (taken as is the practice from the first words of the document) is *Gaudium et spes*: joy and hope. This constitution does give us cause for joy in its breadth and vision. And its practical concern gives us much cause for hope. Most of the space in this slender volume will be given over to the four constitutions and especially to the fourth as being most representative of the spirit of the Council. For more than its teaching, which for the most part is not new, it is the spirit of the Council that we want to get in touch with and let enliven our lives as it changes our perspective and enables us to live out of joy and hope even in the face of "the griefs and the anxieties of the women and men of this age."

The Council's decrees circle around the Dogmatic Constitution concerning Church. The first decree published by the Council is the weakest, though not the least important, and the obvious place to start: the Decree concerning the Instruments of Social Communication (*Inter mirifica*). Jesus said: Go forth and teach all. This is fundamental. It is the way the source, the divine revelation, creates Church. Faith comes from hearing. The contribution of this decree is that it opened the way for the effective instructions in this matter that have followed. Much, very much remains to be done on the part of the People of God to develop our use of the powerful means of communication increasingly available in our times to bring the Good News to all. The decree calls us to the task. Undoubtedly it was the wise disposition of the guiding Spirit that the document itself remained little more than a clarion call, for the rapid development of the media would have quickly reduced anything more concrete to obsolescence. Nonetheless one could wish that this feeble document had been enriched by the deeper reflection of the later sessions of the Council. The Pastoral Constitution concerning Church in the Modern World does return briefly to this very important matter.

Other decrees of the Council sought to give practical direction in regard to those who make up the Church:

- *bishops:* the Decree concerning the Bishops' Pastoral Office in the Church (*Christus Dominus*);

- *priests:* the Decree concerning the Ministry and Life of Priests (*Presbyterorum ordinis*) and the Decree concerning Priestly Formation (*Optatam totius*);

- *laity:* the Decree concerning the Apostolate of the Laity (*Apostolicum actuositatem*);

- *religious,* that group which includes both priests and laity: the Decree on the Appropriate Renewal of the Religious Life (*Perfectae caritatis*).

The makeup of the Church does not end with these persons. This is one of the more significant dimensions of the Dogmatic Constitution concerning Church. And one of the items of "unfinished business" of the Council. The Council, acknowledging a development in doctrine, did not subscribe to the teaching of the recent pope, Pius XII, and identify the Church with the Roman Catholic Church. While it teaches that the Church "subsists" (*subsistit*) in the Catholic Church (only time and much theological reflection will reveal to us just what that rather enigmatic word really means), it acknowledges that the Church's reality extends beyond this institution. The fathers purposefully used a vague word, leaving room for a continuing development of understanding of the extension of the Church within the other Churches and ecclesial communities, among those who are referred to in the Council documents as "the separated brothers and sisters." Thus the Decrees concerning Eastern Catholic Churches (*Orientalium Ecclesiarum*) and Ecumenism (*Unitatis redintegratio*) pertain not only to activities of the Church, as do the Decree concerning the Church's Missionary Activity (*Ad Gentes*) and the Declaration concerning Christian Education (*Gravissimum educationis*), or relations with those not sacramentally baptized into Christ, as does the Declaration concerning the Relationship of the Church to Non-Christian Religions (*Nostra aetate*), but to others who clearly pertain to the Church.

The final document to enter into the consideration of the fathers and the one that created the most excitement was the Declaration concerning Religious Freedom (*Dignitatis humanae*). Those who were looking to the Council for a biblical perspective that was progressive rather than repressive, inclusive and respectful of pluralism instead of exclusive and sectarian, that spoke the language of social justice and personal responsibility and pointed to an economic ethic rooted in the religious requirements of community could find what they were looking for, though in a rather cumbersome way and couched in a certain amount of compromise, in the Pastoral Constitution concerning Church in the Modern World. However it was the much more succinct and direct Declaration concerning Religious Freedom that spoke more to the aspirations of their hearts.

The translations of the documents of the Council offered here follow very closely those edited by Monsignor Joseph Gallagher for Walter Abbott's edition of the Council documents. However not only are they carefully selected portions of the documents but the translations have been re-edited in light of the developments that have taken place in the language of the Church and in American usage since the time the Abbott volume was published. I have for the most part avoided what is called today "sexist" language. I think this is important. We are consciously or unconsciously formed by

what we say and hear and read. The use of masculine forms
to include the feminine conveys attitudes that are undesir-
able, to say the least. However, the fact that Jesus used the
name "Father" when he spoke to God and referred to himself as "the Son" is sufficient warranty for his followers to do
likewise. At the same time I think we can respect the freedom
of those who wish to use the feminine form when referring
to Holy Spirit. When Jesus first spoke of the Spirit he did not
hesitate to use feminine and maternal imagery (John 3:5–8).

We all realize that in the Divine Persons there are no gender differences; the fullness of all the being that masculine
and feminine comprise is present in them as the Source. As
Genesis recounts: "God created man in the image of himself,
in the image of God he created him, male and female he created them." Both male and female image God. It is part of
the poverty of the English language that it does not have an
"utrum" vocabulary, one that embraces both the masculine
and the feminine at the same time. If we find in ourselves
some reactions to the use of the feminine to refer to Holy
Spirit, this might invite us to look at what pre-judgments, if
not prejudices, might be behind this reaction.

The Latin word for Church, *ecclesia,* is feminine. This ac-
counts in part for the common use of feminine references
when speaking of the Church, as does the use of such imagery
as "Spouse" of Christ. However, I have avoided this person-
alization, as it tends to convey the idea that the Church has
an entity apart from us. The fathers of the Council sometimes
fell into this way of thinking and speak of "the Church" addressing itself to the faithful as if the faithful were not the
Church; they are more than 99 percent of it.

It has been difficult to make a selection among the very
many pregnant passages that can be found within the sixteen
documents of the Second Vatican Council. I would have liked
to have included the whole of each and every document as

well as the messages the Council addressed to various segments of the human family, for there is much to be found in them but that would not have served the primary purpose of this volume. I trust the excerpts chosen will not only give the reader the substance of the Council's teaching but give enough taste for the texts that many will want to go on to study the complete documents.

One of the big challenges for us as we open ourselves to these documents, to what they teach and the spirit they seek to impart, is for us to constantly remember that *we are the Church*. The Church was not the Council fathers assembled (though sometimes they spoke as if they saw themselves that way), nor is it the hierarchy spread through the world today. It is not just the head, as important as that member is, and most certainly not those who surround the earthly head at Rome and often dare to speak in his name and in the name of all of us.

We are the Church. That is one of the reasons why the Council is not over, why reception is a vital part of it. As the Council affirms, "The body of the faithful as a whole, anointed as they are by the Holy One, cannot err in matters of belief.... God's People accept not the word of human persons but the very Word of God."

We are the Church. So each time we hear these documents say "the Church," "the People of God," we are rightly challenged to ask ourselves: Is that really me? Is that really us? The answer does not have to always be "yes"; again, this is where reception plays its role. We do not have to say "yes," but we do owe it to the Spirit operative in the Council, to our fellow members, and to ourselves to listen and question and in a spirit of faith seek to understand and accept what the Spirit is saying to the Church. Question, not out of a critical spirit or out of ignorance or a narrow or even closed mindedness. But question with the Spirit living in us, out of our lived experience as living members of the Church. The Spirit spoke in and through the Council to help us become more truly wise and spirit-filled humans who share more fully the mind of Christ as it encounters in us the evolving realities of her continuing creation. If we can face the Council and the challenge it offers in this way then we will indeed know that it is not dead but very much alive. It lives with the living Spirit of Christ, albeit incarnate within a community of sinners (us) replete with all the blindness, stupidity, and limitations that sin brings into our lives, which have not yet fully accepted the redeeming grace and wisdom of Christ.

The Council did not in fact say very much specifically about leadership. Yet I think this is very much what was and is being looked for not only among Catholics but all peoples conscious of the converging world community. We feel deeply the need for leaders who have vision and speak with wisdom in times when there does not seem to be much wisdom abroad, those who can open new worlds for us in their able communication, who will encourage us, truly listening to us and caring. There were such men in the Council. The most outstanding of them were quickly recognized and cast into a role, that of council presidents. And in the end, the Council itself, in spite of its size and spectrum, above all in the document that came forth most immediately from its own heart, the Pastoral Constitution concerning Church in the Modern World, did give to us and to the world such leadership. Unfortunately the leader's voice was even initially somewhat muffled by compromise and has not subsequently ever been broadcast in the powerful way it should be. It is my hope that this volume will help some to hear the Council more clearly and know the joy and hope the hearing of that voice can engender.

1

The People of God

Some say it was the people's council. It gave the Church back to the people. People, ordinary people, were again somebody in the Church. They can do something in the Church.

Others say it was the bishops' council. It was bishops who gathered and they spoke above all about bishops. They clarified their role and affirmed their power albeit as a service to the Church.

Perhaps in truth it was both. We must remember that bishops are people, members of the Church, of the People of God. And like all the others they, too, are subject to the headship of Christ in heaven and his vicar on earth. If a certain tension arises from the role of bishops among the People of God, may it be a healthy, life-giving tension — the tension of a taut bowstring that can send the Church on a powerful trajectory that will eventually arrive at the center of its target, the very heart of God.

Before entering upon its consideration of these two very important and complementary elements of Church, the Dogmatic Constitution concerning Church presents a rich if concise summary of salvation history, culminating, as it does, in

Christ and his Church. Each of the documents of the Second Vatican Council and almost every significant section of them begins with some theological exposition that is usually quite scriptural. These sections are extremely important, for they give us the source, foundation, and context for what is to follow, for the realities and the life of the Church. These need to be prayerfully read and reread and pondered. If the responses that the Revelation gives to the deeper questions of our lives are going to be effectively heard so that they are able to provide a satisfying and hope-inspiring answer, then they have to be heard deeply.

Most of us, unfortunately, first received what the Church with the divine Revelation has to say to us through the pat answers of the catechism. First impressions are lasting impressions. These pat answers presented themselves as *the* answers, all the Church had to say. As our minds developed and questioned more, these pat answers did not satisfy — they could not. We left them behind. And many, taking that to be all that the Church had to offer in the way of responses to life's deeper questions, went on to look elsewhere or gave up hope of finding meaningful answers and went on to live a superficial, materialistic, or hedonistic life.

There are no pat answers. But the Revelation coming through the Church does have much to contribute as we search ever more deeply into the mystery that we are, the meaning of life, of human community, of the world as we experience it. Even as the Word of the Lord invites us to wonder more and more at the magnificence of the reality, it leads us more and more deeply into the question. It is good to live in the question. Pat answers close things down and leave us with little hope. Questions that ever expand and deepen give birth to expansive hope and longing love, give birth to life and that more abundantly.

The Council may seem at first self-preoccupied. In a sense

this is so. And it is right. Let us remember Augustine's prayer: *Noverim me ut noverim te.* May I know myself in order that I might know you. The more we know ourselves, the more we can know God, our Creator. The more we know ourselves, the more we can know and understand our fellow humans — and all the rest of the creation that has been made for us. In seeking to set forth a deeper and fuller perception of Church, the Council is in fact seeking to reveal primarily not itself but Christ. He is the Light of Nations, *Lumen Gentium,* whose radiance brightens the countenance of the Church, the whole Christ who is the unity and fullness of humankind. For the Church is a sacrament.

Dionysius the Pseudo-Areopagite (in fact, a fifth-century Syrian monk) tells us there are three kinds of contemplation: there is *direct* contemplation, which plunges right into the depths of the Reality; there is *oblique* contemplation, which sees the Reality through its reflection in the creation; and there is *circular* contemplation, which looks first at one facet and then at another, gradually gaining a perception of the whole. In this circular fashion the constitution approaches the mystery of Church. It gathers up images from the Revelation: Kingdom of Christ, a people, a little flock of Christ, an initial budding forth of the Kingdom, a sheepfold, vineyard, the edifice of God, the house of God, the household of God, the dwelling place of God among women and men, a holy temple, the Jerusalem that is above, our mother, the spotless lamb, a new creation, mystically Christ's own body, his bride, pillar and mainstay of truth, the new People of God, the messianic people, the instrument of redemption, the Church of Christ, a chosen race, a royal priesthood, a holy nation, a purchased people, a spiritual house ... and invites us through these to garner some perceptions of this great mystery.

We have our sublime dignity, yet paradoxically we are most like Christ when we labor in poverty and oppression.

Christ, the Son of God, was indeed a poor man, and his op-
pressors dogged him until they succeeded in bringing him to
an ignominious death. The option for the poor that is rightly
to be ours is not missing from this basic self-identification of
the Church:

> Just as Christ carried out the work of redemption in poverty and
> under oppression so the Church is called to follow the same path
> in communicating to women and men the fruits of salvation. Christ
> Jesus, "though he was by nature God...emptied himself, taking the
> nature of a slave" (Phil. 2:6), and "being rich, he became poor"
> (2 Cor. 8:9) for our sakes. Thus, although the Church needs human
> resources to carry out its mission, it is not set up to seek earthly
> glory but to proclaim humility and self-sacrifice even by its own ex-
> ample. Christ was sent by the Father "to evangelize the poor...to
> heal the contrite of heart" (Lk. 4:18), "to seek and save what was
> lost" (Lk. 19:10). Similarly the Church embraces with love all those
> who are afflicted with human weakness. Indeed, it recognizes in the
> poor and the suffering the likeness of its poor and suffering Founder.
> It does all it can to relieve their need and in them it strives to serve
> Christ. (Dogmatic Constitution concerning Church, 8)

Alas, even as the fathers speak of our option for the poor a
certain triumphalism creeps in: "It does all it can to relieve
their need...." We the Church do all that we can to relieve
the needs of the poor? Who could believe it? Let us not kid
ourselves. And let us humbly strive to do ever more.

I do not want to say that the document is without a certain humility. But we have these incongruities: at the very
moment the fathers affirm that we the Church are "always
in need of being purified" they claim that the Church "incessantly pursues the path of penance and renewal."[1] Some
of us do some of the time, thanks be to God. But if we the

---

1. In this and in similar cases it may be true that the writers intended more
to express an ideal to be strived for rather than stating a fact. In any case we do
need to be challenged by such statements.

Church as a whole had been incessantly pursuing renewal there would have been no need for a council. The spirituality that the Council calls us to is a spirituality of constant conversion and renewal in living out each our own particular vocation among the People of God.

The Mystery of the Church

1. Christ is the light of the nations. Hence this Synod, which has been gathered in Holy Spirit, eagerly desires to shed on all that radiance of his which brightens the countenance of the Church. This it will do by proclaiming the Gospel to every creature (cf. Mk. 16:15). By its relationship with Christ, the Church is a kind of sacrament or sign of intimate union with God and of the unity of humankind....

2. By an utterly free and mysterious decree of his own wisdom and goodness, the eternal Father created the whole world. His plan was to dignify women and men with a participation in his own divine life. He did not abandon women and men after they had fallen in Adam but ceaselessly offered them helps to salvation in anticipation of Christ the Redeemer.... He planned to assemble in the Church all those who would believe in Christ. Already from the beginning of the world the foreshadowing of the Church took place. It was prepared for in a remarkable way throughout the history of the people of Israel and by means of the Old Covenant. Established in the present era of time, the Church was made manifest by the outpouring of the Spirit. At the end of time it will achieve its glorious fulfillment. Then, as may be read in the holy Fathers, all just persons from the time of Adam ... will be gathered together with the Father in the universal Church.

3. The Son came on mission from his Father. It was in him, before the foundation of the world, that the Father chose us and predestined us to become adopted sons and daughters, for in him it has pleased the Father to re-establish all things (cf. Eph. 1:4–5 and 10). To carry out the will of the Father Christ inaugurated the Kingdom of heaven on earth and revealed to us the mystery of the Father. By his obedience he brought about redemption. The Church or in

other words the Kingdom of Christ now present in mystery grows visibly in the world through the power of God....

4. When the work which the Father had given the Son to do on earth (cf. Jn. 17:4) was accomplished, Holy Spirit was sent on the day of Pentecost in order that she might forever sanctify the Church and thus all believers would have access to the Father through Christ in the one Spirit (cf. Eph. 2:18). She is the spirit of life, a fountain of water springing up to life eternal (cf. Jn. 4:14; 7:38-39). Through her the Father gives life to women and men who are dead from sin, till at last she revives in Christ even their mortal bodies (cf. Rom. 8:10-11)....

5. The mystery of Church is manifest in its very foundation, for the Lord Jesus inaugurated it by preaching the Good News, that is, the coming of God's Kingdom which for centuries had been promised in the Scriptures: "The time is fulfilled and the Kingdom of God is at hand" (Mk. 1:15; cf. Mt. 4:17). In Christ's word, in his works, and in his presence this Kingdom reveals itself to women and men....

6. In the Old Testament the revelation of the Kingdom had often been conveyed by figures of speech. In the same way the inner nature of the Church is made known to us through various images made ready to serve this purpose in the books of the Prophets — images drawn from pastoral life, agriculture, building construction, and even from family and married life.

Thus, the Church is a sheepfold whose one and necessary door is Christ (Jn. 10:1-10). It is a flock of which God himself foretold that he would be the Shepherd (cf. Is. 40:11; Ez. 32:11 ff.). Although guided by human shepherds, its sheep are nevertheless ceaselessly led and nourished by Christ himself, the Good Shepherd and the Prince of Pastors (cf. Jn. 10:11; 1 Pet. 5:4), who gave his life for the sheep (cf. Jn. 10:10-15).

The Church is a tract of land to be cultivated, the field of God (1 Cor. 3:9). On that land grows the ancient olive tree whose holy roots were the Patriarchs and in which the reconciliation of Jew and Gentile has been brought about and will be brought about (Rom. 11:13-26). The Church has been cultivated by the heavenly Vinedresser as his choice vineyard (Mt. 21:33–43 par.; cf. Is. 5:1ff.). The true vine is Christ who gives life and fruitfulness to the branches, that is, to us. Through the Church we abide in Christ without whom we can do nothing (Jn. 15:1–5).

The Church has more often been called the edifice of God (1 Cor. 3:9). Even the Lord himself likened himself to the stone which the builders rejected but which became the cornerstone (Mt. 21:42 par.; cf. Acts 4:11; 1 Pet. 2:7; Ps. 117:22). On this foundation the Church is built by the apostles (cf. 1 Cor. 3:11) and from it the Church receives durability and solidity. This edifice is adorned by various names: the house of God (1 Tim. 3:15) in which dwells his family; the household of God in the Spirit (cf. Rev. 21:3); and, especially, the holy temple. This temple, symbolized by places of worship built out of stone, is praised by the holy Fathers and, not without reason, is compared in the liturgy to the Holy City, the New Jerusalem.[2] As living stones we here on earth are being built up along with this City (1 Pet. 2:5). John contemplates this Holy City coming down out of heaven from God, when the world is made new and prepared like a bride for her husband (Rev. 21:1f.).

The Church, "that Jerusalem which is above," is also called "our mother" (Gal. 4:26; cf. Rev. 12:17). It is described as the spotless bride of the spotless Lamb (Rev. 19:7; 21:2 and 9; 22:17). The Church it was whom Christ "loved and delivered himself up for that he might sanctify it" (Eph. 5:26), whom he united to himself by an unbreakable covenant and whom he unceasingly "nourishes and cherishes" (Eph. 5:29). Once it had been purified, he willed it to be joined to himself and to be subject to him in love and fidelity (cf. Eph. 5:24). Finally, he filled it with heavenly gifts which will last for all eternity in order that we might know the love of God and of Christ for us, a love which surpasses all knowledge (cf. Eph. 3:19). The Church on earth, while journeying in a foreign land away from its Lord (cf. 2 Cor. 5:6), regards itself as an exile. Hence it seeks and savors those things which are above, where Christ is seated at the right hand of God, where the life of the Church is hidden with Christ in God until it appears in glory with its Spouse (cf. Col. 3:1–4).

---

2. Origen, *On Matthew,* 16, 21; Tertullian, *Against Mark,* 3, 7.

7. In the human nature which he united to himself, the Son of God redeemed women and men and transformed them into new creatures (cf. Gal. 6:15; 2 Cor. 5:17) by overcoming death through his own death and resurrection. By communicating his Spirit to his brothers and sisters called together from all peoples, Christ made them mystically into his own body.

As all the members of the human body, though they are many, form one body, so also are the faithful in Christ (cf. 1 Cor. 12:12). Also, in the building up of Christ's body, a variety of members and functions comes forth. There is one Spirit who, according to her own richness and the needs of the ministries, distributes her different gifts for the welfare of the Church (cf. 1 Cor. 12:1–11). Among those gifts stands out the grace given to the apostles. To their authority the Spirit herself subjected even those who were endowed with charisms (cf. 1 Cor. 14)....

8. Christ, the one Mediator, established and ceaselessly sustains here on earth his holy Church, the community of faith, hope, and charity, as a visible structure. Through it he communicates truth and grace to all. But the society furnished with hierarchical agencies and the Mystical Body of Christ are not to be considered as two realities nor are the visible assembly and the spiritual community nor the earthly Church and the Church enriched with heavenly things. Rather they form one interlocked reality which is comprised of a divine and a human element. For this reason, by an excellent analogy, this reality is compared to the mystery of the incarnate Word. Just as the assumed nature inseparably united to the divine Word serves him as a living instrument of salvation so, in a similar way, does the communal structure of the Church serve Christ's Spirit, who vivifies it, in building up the body (cf. Eph. 4:16).

This is the unique Church of Christ which in the Creed we avow as one, holy, catholic, and apostolic. After his resurrection our Savior handed it over to Peter to be shepherded (Jn. 21:17), commissioning him and the other apostles to propagate and govern it (cf. Mt. 28:18 ff.). It he erected for all ages as "the pillar and mainstay of the truth" (1 Tim. 3:15). This church, constituted and organized in the world as a society, subsists in the Catholic Church, which is governed by the successor of Peter and by the bishops in union with that successor. Nevertheless many elements of sanctification and of truth can be found outside of its visible structure....

With the Council there came a fundamental shift in the magisterium's basic perception of ourselves as Church. Prior to the Council, ecclesiology was culminating in the analogy of the Mystical Body of Christ. We have only to think of Pius XII's encyclical of that name published a short time before. Mystical Body is a tightly contained image. There is only one head, Christ in heaven with his vicar on earth. The parameters are very clear — it has all the distinctness of a body. But with the Council there emerged a much fuller, richer, and more fluid notion: the People of God. We are a vast throng, led not only by a head but by a large group of leaders, equally called to this by Christ. The defining edges of Church are not so clear. Church does "subsist" in the Roman Catholic Church.

This Church, constituted and organized in the world as a society, subsists in the Catholic Church which is governed by the successor of Peter and by the bishops in union with that successor.... (8)

Theologians for decades to come are going to have fun working with that word, "subsist," chosen by the fathers of the Council precisely because it is open to various interpretations. The fathers very deliberately left room for the development of doctrine. In any case they make it clear that Church exists among our fellow Christians of other Churches and ecclesial communities. They reach further and speak of its presence among our Jewish brothers and sisters, among the Moslems, among the faithful of still other, theologically more distant, religious communities, and even among those who hold to no faith whatsoever yet respond to the truth.

This is not something wholly new or novel. Our traditional teaching has held that there are three kinds of baptism:
baptism of water — the sacrament celebrated in most of
the Christian Churches; baptism of blood — the shedding
of one's blood for one's faith; and baptism of desire. This
last meant that anyone who said "yes" to the truth as he or
she honestly perceived it would receive the baptismal graces
of Christ. For Christ is the Truth. Unfortunately, this older,
more traditional way of presenting this reality was sensed by
others as being somewhat imperialistic. The faithful, believing Moslem does not see himself or herself as coming into
the baptismal grace of Christ. Our Moslem friend can more
readily identify with the new image of a People of God. Yes,
we are together in some way, all of us, as the People of God.

The People of God

9. At all times and among every people God has welcomed who-
ever fears him and does what is right (cf. Acts 10:35). It has pleased
God, however, to make women and men holy and save them not
merely as individuals without any mutual bonds but by making them
into a single people, a people which acknowledges him in truth and
serves him in holiness. He therefore chose the race of Israel as a
people unto himself. With it he set up a covenant. Step by step
he taught this people. Through its unfolding history he manifested
himself and the decree of his will. He made it a people holy unto
himself. All these things, however, were done by way of preparation
and as a figure of that new and perfect covenant which was to be
ratified in Christ, of that more luminous revelation which was to be
given through God's very Word made flesh. . . .

Christ instituted this new covenant, that is to say, the new testament in his blood (cf. 1 Cor. 11:25) by calling together a people
made up of Jew and Gentile, making them one not according to the
flesh but in the Spirit.

This was to be the new People of God. For those who believe in Christ, who are reborn not from a perishable but from an imperishable seed through the Word of the living God (cf. 1 Pet. 1:23), not from the flesh but from water and Holy Spirit (cf. Jn. 3:5–6), are finally established as "a chosen race, a royal priesthood, a holy nation, a purchased people.... You who in times past were not a people are now the people of God" (1 Pet. 2:9–10).

That messianic people has for its head Christ "who was delivered up for our sins and rose again for our justification" (Rom. 4:25) and who now, having won a name which is above all names, reigns in glory in heaven. The heritage of this people are the dignity and freedom of the sons and daughters of God in whose hearts Holy Spirit dwells as in her temple. Its law is the new commandment to love as Christ loves us (cf. Jn. 13:34). Its goal is the Kingdom of God, which has been begun by God himself on earth and which is to be further extended until it is brought to perfection by him at the end of time....

Established by Christ as a fellowship of life, charity, and truth, it is also used by him as an instrument for the redemption of all and is sent forth into the whole world as the light of the world and the salt of the earth (cf. Mt. 5:13–16)....

While it transcends all limits of time and race, the Church is destined to extend to all regions of the earth and so to enter into the history of humankind....

A Priestly People

10. Christ the Lord, High Priest taken from among women and men (cf. Heb. 5:1–5), "made a kingdom and priests to God his Father" (Rev. 1:6; cf. 5:9–10) out of this new people....

Though they differ from one another in essence and not only in degree, the common priesthood of the faithful and the ministerial or hierarchical priesthood are nonetheless interrelated. Each of them in its own special way is a participation in the one priesthood of Christ. The ministerial priest, by the sacred power he enjoys, molds and rules the priestly people. Acting in the person of Christ, he brings about the Eucharistic Sacrifice and offers it to God in the name of all the people. For their part the faithful join in the offering of the Eucharist by virtue of their royal priesthood. They likewise exercise that priesthood by receiving the sacraments, by prayer and thanksgiving, by the witness of a holy life, and by self-denial and active charity.

11. It is through the sacraments and the exercise of the virtues that the sacred nature and organic structure of the priestly community is brought into operation. Incorporated into the Church through baptism, the faithful are consecrated by the baptismal character to enter into Christian worship. Reborn as daughters and sons of God, let them confess before women and men the faith which they have received from God through the Church. Bound more intimately to the Church by the sacrament of confirmation, they are endowed by Holy Spirit with special strength. Hence they are more strictly bound to spread and defend the faith both by word and by deed as true witnesses of Christ.

Taking part in the Eucharistic Sacrifice, which is the fount and apex of the whole Christian life, they offer the divine Victim to God and offer themselves along with him. Thus, both by the act of oblation and through holy communion, all perform their proper part in this liturgical service, not, indeed, all in the same way but each in that way which is appropriate to one's self. Strengthened anew at the holy table by the Body of Christ, they manifest in a practical way that unity of God's People which is suitably signified and wondrously brought about by this most awesome sacrament.

Those who approach the sacrament of penance obtain pardon from the mercy of God for offenses committed against him. They are at the same time reconciled with the Church, which they have wounded by their sins, and which by charity, example, and prayer seeks their conversion. By the sacred anointing of the sick and the prayer of the priests, the whole Church commends those who are ill to the suffering and glorified Lord, asking that he may lighten their sufferings and save them (cf. Jas. 5:14–16).... Those of the faithful who are consecrated by holy orders are appointed to feed the Church in Christ's name with the Word and the grace of God.

Finally, Christian couples, in virtue of the sacrament of matrimony, signify and partake of the mystery of that unity and fruitful love which exists between Christ and his Church (cf. Eph. 5:32). The couple thereby help each other to attain to holiness in their married life and by the rearing and education of their children. And so, in their state and way of life, they have their own special gift among the People of God (cf. 1 Cor. 7:7).

For from the marriage of Christians there comes the family in which new citizens of human society are born. By the grace of Holy Spirit received in baptism these are made children of God, thus perpetuating the People of God through the centuries. The family is, we can say, the domestic Church. In it let parents by their word and example be the first preachers of the faith to their children. Let them encourage them in the vocation which is proper to each of them, fostering with special care any religious vocation.

Fortified by so many and such powerful means of salvation, all the faithful, whatever their condition or state, are called by the Lord, each in his or her own way, to that perfect holiness whereby the Father himself is perfect.

A Prophetic People

12. The holy People of God share also in Christ's prophetic office. It spreads abroad a living witness to him, especially by means of a life of faith and charity and by offering to God a sacrifice of praise, the tribute of lips which give honor to his name (cf. Heb. 13:15). The body of the faithful as a whole, anointed as they are by the Holy One (cf. Jn. 2:20, 27), cannot err in matters of belief. Thanks to a supernatural sense of the faith which characterizes the People as a whole, it manifests this unerring quality when, "from the bishops down to the last member of the laity,"[3] it shows universal agreement in matters of faith and morals.

For by this sense of faith which is aroused and sustained by the Spirit of truth, God's People accept not the word of human persons

---

3. St. Augustine, *Concerning Holy Preaching*, 14, 27.

but the very Word of God (cf. 1 Th. 2:13). They cling without fail to the faith once delivered to the saints (cf. Jude 3), penetrate it more deeply by accurate insights, and apply it more thoroughly to life. All this they do under the lead of a sacred teaching authority to which they loyally defer.

It is not only through the sacraments and Church ministries that the same Holy Spirit sanctifies and leads the People of God and enriches them with virtues. Allotting her gifts "in everyone according as she wills" (1 Cor. 12:11), she distributes special graces among the faithful of every rank. By these gifts she makes them fit and ready to undertake the various tasks or offices advantageous for the renewal and upbuilding of the Church according to the words of the Apostle: "The manifestation of the Spirit is given to everyone for profit" (1 Cor. 12:7). These charismatic gifts, whether they be the most outstanding or the more simple and widely diffused, are to be received with thanksgiving and consolation, for they are exceedingly suitable and useful for the needs of the Church....

The Universality of the Church:
A Communion of All Good People

13. Every member of the human family is called to belong to the new People of God. Wherefore this People, while remaining one and unique, is to be spread throughout the whole world....

It follows that among all the nations of earth there is but one People of God, which takes its citizens from every race, making them citizens of a Kingdom which is of a heavenly and not an earthly nature. For all the faithful scattered throughout the world are in communion with each other in Holy Spirit so that "he who occupies the See of Rome knows the people of India are his members."[4] Since the Kingdom of Christ is not of this world (cf. Jn. 18:36) the Church or People of God take nothing away from the temporal welfare of any people by establishing that Kingdom. Rather it fos-

---

4. St. John Chrysostom, *Homilies concerning St. John's Gospel,* 65, 1.

ters and takes to itself, insofar as they are good, the abilities and resources and customs of each people....

Not only, then, is the People of God made up of different peoples but even in its inner structure it is composed of various ranks. This diversity among its members arises either by reason of their duties, as is the case with those who exercise the sacred ministry for the good of their brothers and sisters, or by reason of their situation and way of life, as is the case with these many who enter the religious state and, tending toward holiness by a narrower path, stimulate their sisters and brothers by their example.

Moreover, within the Church particular Churches hold a rightful place. These Churches retain their own tradition without in any way lessening the primacy of the Chair of Peter. This Chair presides over the whole assembly of charity and protects legitimate differences while at the same time it sees that such differences do not hinder unity but rather contribute toward it. Finally, between all the parts of the Church there remains a bond of close communion with respect to spiritual riches, apostolic workers, and temporal resources. For the members of the People of God are called to share these goods. To each of the Churches the words of the Apostle apply: "According to the gift that each has received, administer it to one another as good stewards of the manifold grace of God" (1 Pet. 4:10).

All are called to be part of this universal unity of the People of God, which foretells and promises universal peace. And they belong to it or are related to it in various ways, the Catholic faithful, others who believe in Christ, and indeed the whole of humankind, called to salvation by the grace of God.

...the Catholic Faithful

14. This Synod turns its attention first to the Catholic faithful. Basing itself upon sacred Scriptures and Tradition, it teaches that the Church, now sojourning on earth as an exile, is necessary for salvation. For the one Christ, made present to us in his Body which is the Church, is Mediator and the way of salvation. In explicit terms he himself affirmed the necessity of faith and baptism (cf. Mk. 16:16;

Jn. 3:5) and thereby affirmed also the necessity of the Church, for through baptism as through a door one enters the Church. Whosoever, therefore, knowing that the Catholic Church was made necessary by God through Jesus Christ, would refuse to enter it or to remain in it cannot be saved.

They are fully incorporated into the society of the Church who, possessing the Spirit of Christ, accept its entire ordering and all the means of salvation given it and through union with its visible structure are joined to Christ, who rules it through the Supreme Pontiff and the bishops. This joining is effected by the bonds of professed faith, sacraments, ecclesiastical government, and communion. Those are not saved, however, who though they are incorporated in the Church do not persevere in charity. They remain indeed in the Church "bodily" but not according to the "heart." All the daughters and sons of the Church should remember that their special status is to be attributed not to their own merits but to the special grace of Christ. If they fail moreover to respond to that grace in thought, word, and deed, not only will they not be saved but they will be the more severely judged.

...the Catechumens

Catechumens who, moved by Holy Spirit, seek with explicit intention to be incorporated into the Church are by that very intention joined to it....

...all Baptized Christians

15. The Church recognizes that in many ways it is linked with those who, being baptized, are honored with the name Christian, though they do not profess the faith in its entirety or do not preserve unity of communion with the successor of Peter. For there are many who honor sacred Scripture, taking it as the norm of belief, and who show a true religious zeal. They lovingly believe in God the Father Almighty and in Christ, Son of God and Savior. They are consecrated by baptism, through which they are united with Christ.

They also recognize and receive other sacraments within their own Churches or ecclesial communities. Many of them rejoice in the episcopate, celebrate the Holy Eucharist, and cultivate devotion toward the Virgin Mother of God. They also share with us in prayer and other spiritual benefits.

Likewise, we can say that in some real way they are joined with us in Holy Spirit, for to them also she gives her gifts and graces and is thereby operative among them with her sanctifying power. Some indeed she has strengthened to the extent of the shedding of their blood.

...Jews, Moslems, All Who Say "Yes" to the Truth

16. Finally, those who have not yet received the Gospel are related in various ways to the People of God. In the first place there is the people to whom the covenants and the promises were given and from whom Christ was born according to the flesh (cf. Rom. 9:4–5). On account of their fathers this people remains most dear to God, for God does not repent of the gifts he makes nor of the calls he issues (cf. Rom. 11:28–29).

But the plan of salvation also includes those who acknowledge the Creator. In the first place among these are the Moslems who, professing to hold the faith of Abraham, along with us adore the one and merciful God who on the last day will judge humankind. Nor is God himself far distant from those who in shadows and images seek the unknown God, for it is he who gives to all life and breath and every other gift (cf. Acts 17:25–28) and who as Savior wills that all be saved (cf. 1 Tim. 2:4).

Those also can attain to everlasting salvation who through no fault of their own do not know the Gospel of Christ or his Church yet sincerely seek God and, moved by grace, strive by their deeds to do his will as it is known to them through the dictates of conscience. Nor does divine Providence deny the help necessary for salvation to those who without blame on their part have not yet arrived at an explicit knowledge of God but who strive to live a good life thanks to his grace....

A People with a Mission

17. Just as the Son was sent by the Father, so he too sent the Apostles (cf. Jn. 20:21), saying: "Go, therefore, and make disciples of all nations, baptizing them in the name of the Father and of the Son and of Holy Spirit, teaching them to observe all that I have commanded you; and behold, I am with you all days even unto the consummation of the world" (Mt. 28:18–20).

The Church has received from the Apostles as a task to be discharged even to the ends of the earth this solemn mandate of Christ to proclaim the saving truth (cf. Acts 1:8). Hence it makes the words of the Apostles its own: "Woe to me if I do not preach the Gospel" (1 Cor. 9:16) and continues unceasingly to send heralds of the Gospel until such time as the infant Churches are fully established and can themselves carry on the work of evangelizing....

The obligation of spreading the faith is imposed on every disciple of Christ, according to each one's ability....

Church is present wherever there is a gathering of the People of God. Church exists in the Churches. The bishops, dispersed throughout the world, each head a local Church. And these local Churches together form the Catholic Church.

In and from such individual Churches there comes into being the one and only Catholic Church. (23)

The principle of collegiality continues to flow down from there. The local Church of the bishop is made up of all the parochial Churches dispersed through the diocese. The pastors are his college, each member heading a more local Church. Even within the parish, the pastor needs to call forth his college of leaders. A parish is truly what it should be only when every member of that parish is enfolded in a group small enough for each member to care for the others and be cared for by them. Within the parish we need all kinds of groups: prayer groups (centering prayer, rosary, charismatic prayer), study groups, apostolic groups, youth groups, parents groups, senior citizens, twelve-step groups, Legion of Mary. The particular group may gather for a particular purpose but the more important thing that will happen is that the members will, through their regular meetings, bond and truly form Church. Again, a parish is truly what it should be only when every member of that parish is enfolded in a group small enough for each member to care for the others and be cared for by them. And the leaders of these groups with the pastor and under his headship will lead this portion of the People of God, the Church.

There remains a special headship in the college of bishops, the college that is the direct successor of the apostolic college established by Christ himself. As such the bishops share in a special way in the threefold mission of the Lord to teach, sanctify, and govern. The Council saw the bishop's duty to preach as occupying "an eminent role." The constitution goes on to say:

In matters of faith and morals the bishops speak in the name of Christ and the faithful are to accept their teaching and adhere to it with a religious assent of soul. (25)

The text refers this most especially to the teachings of the Bishop of Rome, and that when he is not speaking infallibly or, as they say, *ex cathedra,* speaking from the chair of Peter. Infallible pronouncements are few and far between. They are in themselves usually not the problem for most of the faithful. But what does a "religious assent of soul" call for in regards to fallible pronouncements — for if something is not infallible it is necessarily fallible, capable of being wrong? The constitution goes on to explain this to some extent, for it is a matter that has long been discussed. It says (referring in this instance to the Bishop of Rome in particular):

...his magisterium is acknowledged with reverence, the judgments made by him are sincerely adhered to, according to his manifest mind and will. His mind and will in the matter may be known chiefly either from the character of the documents, from his frequent repetition of the same doctrine, or from his manner of speaking. (25)

The bishops' right, duty, and service to teach in matters of faith and morals is easily enough acknowledged and with reverence. The mind and heart or will of the believer enter in, for it is an assent given in faith. The adhesion to what the pope or the college of bishops actually teaches in a particular instance is to be responsive to the certitude with which they teach the matter at hand. If the pronouncement is given with the infallible authority that resides within the college as a whole or with the pope "in virtue of his office, when, as the supreme shepherd and teacher of all faithful, he confirms his brothers and sisters in their faith," then it requires our unconditional adhesion. If the matter is not set forth with that same infallible certitude then there is room for the religious mind to deeply weigh the teaching in coming to its assent.

A good Catholic woman or man can religiously acknowledge that the teaching authority of the Church teaches a certain matter with a degree of certitude, though something less than infallibility, and at the same time in the light of his or her own deepest searching find the teaching not to be a certain and sure guide for living a Christ life. Just as the assent in faith given to an infallible or *de fide* pronouncement is a personal responsibility of the faithful person so is the religious assent of soul given to a non-infallible or fallible pronouncement. The "yes" given to the latter should not be the same as that given to the infallible teaching. If it is truly to be an assent of soul, we have to use our minds in making it. This includes our responsibility to develop a fully informed conscience, to seek to understand fully the wisdom being set forth by a teacher guided by Holy Spirit and wise with the wisdom of the ages. The matter may not always be as simple and clear as we might like it to be for our comfort. But that may be as true for the teacher as for the ones taught.

In its deeper perception of the collegial nature of the Church leadership, the Council brought forth a renewed understanding of the Sacrament of Orders, the constituting of ministerial priesthood. Because ministerial priesthood was seen almost totally in terms of leading the Church community at Eucharist, the perception had been that the sacrament was essentially received at the ordination of the priest. The "consecration" of a bishop was something added. Now it is realized that the bishops as successors to the apostles are truly ordained to ministry, Eucharistic indeed, but in its full context of life. Priests, as forming part of the local bishop's college, receive a sharing in his priesthood. This shift has left priests wondering somewhat about their identity in Church. The Council tried to address itself to this question in some subsequent decrees, and we will come back to it.

The Hierarchical Structure of the Church

18. For the nurturing and constant growth of the People of God, Christ the Lord instituted in his Church a variety of ministries, which work for the good of the whole Body. For those ministers who are endowed with sacred power are servants of their brothers and sisters, so that all who are of the People of God and therefore enjoy a true Christian dignity can work toward a common goal freely and in an orderly way and arrive at salvation.

This most sacred Synod, following the footsteps of the First Vatican Council, teaches and declares with that Council that Jesus Christ, the eternal Shepherd, established his holy Church by sending forth the Apostles as he himself had been sent by the Father (cf. Jn. 20:21). He willed that their successors, namely, the bishops, should be shepherds in his Church even to the consummation of the world.

In order that the episcopate itself might be one and undivided he placed blessed Peter over the other Apostles and instituted in him a permanent and visible source and foundation of unity of faith and fellowship. And all this teaching about the institution, the perpetuity, the force and reason for the sacred primacy of the Roman Pontiff and of his infallible teaching authority, this Synod again proposes to be firmly believed by all the faithful.

19. The Lord Jesus, after praying to the Father and calling to himself those whom he desired, appointed twelve men who would stay in his company and whom he would send to preach the Kingdom of God (cf. Mk. 3:13-19; Mt. 10:1-42). These Apostles (cf. Lk. 6:13) he formed after the manner of a college or a fixed group over which he placed Peter chosen from among them (cf. Jn. 21:15-17). He sent them first to the children of Israel and then to all nations (cf. Rom. 1:16) so that as sharers in his power they might make all peoples his disciples, sanctifying and governing them (cf. Mt. 28:16-20; Mk. 16:15; Lk. 24:45-48; Jn. 20:21-23). Thus they would spread his Church and by ministering to it under the guidance of the Lord would shepherd it all days even to the consummation of the world (cf. Mt. 28:20).

They were fully confirmed in this mission on the day of Pentecost (cf. Acts 2:1-26) in accordance with the Lord's promise: "You shall receive power when Holy Spirit comes upon you and you shall be witnesses for me in Jerusalem and in all Judea and in Samaria and even to the very ends of the earth" (Acts 1:8). By everywhere preaching the Gospel (cf. Mk. 16:20), which was accepted by their hearers under the influence of Holy Spirit, the Apostles gathered together the universal Church, which the Lord established on the Apostles and built upon blessed Peter, their chief, Christ Jesus himself remaining the supreme cornerstone (cf. Rev. 21:14; Mt. 16:18; Eph. 2:20).

20. That divine mission entrusted by Christ to the Apostles will last until the end of the world (Mt. 28:20) since the Gospel which was to be handed down by them is for all time the source of all life

for the Church. For this reason the Apostles took care to appoint successors in this hierarchically structured society....

With their helpers, the priests and deacons, bishops have therefore taken up the service of the community, presiding in the place of God over the flock whose shepherd they are, as teachers of doctrine, priests of sacred worship, and ministers of governance....

21. In the bishops, therefore, for whom priests are assistants, our Lord Jesus Christ, the supreme High Priest, is present in the midst of those who believe....

For the discharging of such great duties, the Apostles were enriched by Christ with a special outpouring of Holy Spirit, who came upon them (cf. Acts 1:8; 2:4; Jn. 20:22-23). This spiritual gift they passed on to their helpers by the imposition of hands (cf. 1 Tim. 4:14; 2 Tim. 1:6-7) and it has been transmitted down to us in episcopal consecration. This Synod teaches that by episcopal consecration is conferred the fullness of the sacrament of orders....

Episcopal consecration, together with the office of sanctifying, also confers the office of teaching and of governing. These, however, of their very nature can be exercised only in hierarchical communion with the head and the members of the college. For from tradition, which is expressed especially in liturgical rites and in the practice of the Church both of the East and the West, it is clear that by means of the imposition of hands and the words of consecration the grace of Holy Spirit is so conferred and the sacred character so impressed that bishops in an eminent and visible way undertake Christ's own role as Teacher, Shepherd, and High Priest, and that they act in his person. Therefore it devolves on the bishops to admit newly elected members into the episcopal body by means of the sacrament of orders.

The College of Bishops

22. Just as, by the Lord's will, St. Peter and the other Apostles constituted one apostolic college, so in a similar way the Roman Pontiff as the successor of Peter and the bishops as the successors of the Apostles are joined together. The collegial nature and

meaning of the episcopal order found expression in the very ancient practice by which bishops appointed the world over were
linked with one another and with the Bishop of Rome by the
bonds of unity, charity, and peace; also in the conciliar assemblies
which made common judgments about more profound matters in
decisions reflecting the view of many. The ecumenical councils
held through the centuries clearly attest this collegial aspect. It is
suggested also in the practice introduced in ancient times of sum-
moning several bishops to take part in the elevation of someone
newly elected to the ministry of the high priesthood. Hence, one is
constituted a member of the episcopal body by virtue of sacramental consecration and by Hierarchical communion with the head and
members of the body.

But the college or body of bishops has no authority unless it is
simultaneously conceived of in terms of its head, the Roman Pontiff,
Peter's successor, and without any lessening of his power of primacy
over all, pastors as well as the general faithful. For in virtue of his
office, that is, as Vicar of Christ and pastor of the whole Church,
the Roman Pontiff has full, supreme, and universal power over the
Church. And he can always exercise this power freely....

It is definite, however, that the power of binding and loosing,
which was given to Peter (Mt. 16:19) was granted also to the college of apostles, joined with their head (Mt. 18:18; 28:16–20). This
college, insofar as it is composed of many, expressed the variety
and universality of the People of God, but insofar as it is assembled
under one head, it expresses the unity of the flock of Christ. In it
the bishops, faithfully recognizing the primacy and pre-eminence of
their head, exercise their own authority for the good of their own
faithful and indeed of the whole Church with Holy Spirit constantly
strengthening its organic structure and inner harmony.

The supreme authority over the whole Church with which this
college is empowered is exercised in a solemn way through an ecumenical council. A council is never ecumenical unless it is confirmed
or at least accepted as such by the successor of Peter. It is the prerogative of the Roman Pontiff to convoke these Councils, to preside
over them, and to confirm them. The same collegiate power can be

exercised in union with the pope by the bishops living in all parts of the world, provided that the head of the college calls them to collegiate action or at least so approves or freely accepts the united action of the dispersed bishops that it is made a true collegiate act.

Individual Bishops

23. This collegial union is apparent also in the mutual relations of the individual bishops with particular Churches and with the universal Church. The Roman Pontiff as the successor of Peter is the perpetual and visible source and foundation of the unity of the bishops and of the multitude of the faithful. The individual bishop, however, is the visible principle and foundation of unity in his particular Church, fashioned after the model of the universal Church. In and from such individual Churches there comes into being the one and only Catholic Church....

The individual bishops, who are placed in charge of particular Churches, exercise their pastoral government over the portion of the People of God committed to their care and not over other Churches nor over the universal Church. But each of them as a member of the episcopal college and a legitimate successor of the Apostles is obliged by Christ's decree and command to be solicitous for the whole Church....

24. The canonical mission of the bishops can come about by legitimate customs which have not been revoked by the supreme and universal authority of the Church or by laws made or recognized by that same authority or directly through the successor of Peter himself. If the latter refuses or denies apostolic communion, a bishop cannot assume office.

The Teaching Authority of the Bishops

25. Among the principal duties of bishops, the preaching of the Gospel occupies an eminent place.... Bishops, teaching in communion with the Roman Pontiff, are to be respected by all as witnesses to divine and Catholic truth. In matters of faith and morals, the bish-

ops speak in the name of Christ and the faithful are to accept their teaching and adhere to it with a religious assent of soul. This religious submission of will and of mind must be shown in a special way to the authentic teaching of the Roman Pontiff even when he is not speaking ex *cathedra.*[5] That is, it must be shown in such a way that his supreme magisterium is acknowledged with reverence, the judgments made by him sincerely adhered to, according to his manifest mind and will. His mind and will in the matter may be known chiefly either from the character of the documents, from his frequent repetition of the same doctrine, or from his manner of speaking.

Although the individual bishops do not enjoy the prerogative of infallibility, they can nevertheless proclaim Christ's doctrine infallibly. This is so, even when they are dispersed around the world, provided that while maintaining the bond of unity among themselves and with Peter's successor and while teaching authentically on a matter of faith or morals, they concur in a single viewpoint as the one which must be held conclusively. This authority is even more clearly verified when, gathered together in an ecumenical council, they are teachers and judges of faith and morals for the universal Church. Their definitions must then be adhered to with the submission of faith.

Infallibility

This infallibility with which the divine Redeemer willed his Church to be endowed in defining a doctrine of faith and morals extends as far as extends the deposit of divine revelation, which must be religiously guarded and faithfully expounded. This is the infallibility which the Roman Pontiff, the head of the college of bishops, enjoys in virtue of his office when as the supreme shepherd and teacher of all the faithful who confirms his brothers and sisters in their faith (cf. Lk. 22:32), he proclaims by a definitive act some doctrine of faith

---

5. *Ex cathedra*, which literally means "from his episcopal throne" is a traditional way of expressing those instances when the pope teaches invoking his charism to do so infallibly.

E.C. orded the E. of I., a solemn act therefore infallible, 1st class

or morals. Therefore his definitions of themselves and not from the consent of the Church are justly styled irreformable, for they are pronounced with the assistance of Holy Spirit, an assistance promised him in blessed Peter. Therefore they need no approval of others, nor do they allow an appeal to any other judgment. For then the Roman Pontiff is not pronouncing judgment as a private person. Rather as the supreme teacher of the universal Church as one in whom the charism of the infallibility of the Church itself is individually present, he is expounding or defending a doctrine of Catholic faith.

The infallibility promised to the Church resides also in the body of bishops when the body exercises supreme teaching authority with the successor of Peter. To the resultant definitions the assent of the Church can never be wanting on account of the activity of that same Holy Spirit, whereby the whole flock of Christ is preserved and progresses in unity of faith.

But when either the Roman Pontiff or the Body of Bishops together with him defines a matter, they set it forth in accord with Revelation itself....

But they do not allow that there could be any new public revelation pertaining to the divine deposit of faith....

The Local Church, the Diocese

26. ...This Church of Christ is truly present in all legitimate local congregations of the faithful which, united with their pastors, are themselves called Churches in the New Testament. For in their own locality these are the new people called by God in Holy Spirit and in much fullness (cf. 1 Th. 1:5). In them the faithful are gathered together by the preaching of the Gospel of Christ, and the mystery of the Lord's Supper is celebrated "that by the flesh and blood of the Lord's body the whole brother- and sisterhood may be joined together."[6]

In any community existing around an altar under the sacred ministry of the bishop, there is manifested a symbol of that charity and

---

6. From a Mozarabic prayer.

"unity of the Mystical Body, without which there can be no salvation."[7] In these communities, though frequently small and poor or
living far from any other, Christ is present. By virtue of him the one,
holy, catholic, and apostolic Church gathers together. For "the par-
taking of the Body and Blood of Christ does nothing other than
transform us into that which we consume."[8]

27. Bishops govern the particular Churches entrusted to them as
the vicars and ambassadors of Christ. This they do by their counsel,
exhortations, and example as well as by their authority and sacred
power. This power they use only to build up their flock in truth and
holiness, remembering that he who is greater should become as the
lesser and he who is the more distinguished as the servant (cf. Lk.
22:26-27)....

Nor are they to be regarded as vicars of the Roman Pontiff for
they exercise an authority which is proper to them.... Since he is
sent by the Father to govern his family, a bishop must keep before
his eyes the example of the Good Shepherd who came not to be
ministered unto but to minister (cf. Mt. 20:28; Mk. 10:45) and to lay
down his life for his sheep (cf. Jn. 10:11). Taken from among men
and women and himself beset with weakness, he is able to have
compassion on the ignorant and erring (cf. Heb. 5:1-2). Let him not
refuse to listen to his subjects....

Priests

28. ...Although priests do not possess the highest degree of the
priesthood and although they are dependent on the bishops in the
exercise of their power, they are nevertheless united with the bishops in sacerdotal dignity. By the power of the sacrament of orders
and in the image of Christ the eternal High Priest (Heb. 5:1-10;
7:24; 9:11-28), they are consecrated to preach the Gospel, shepherd the faithful, and celebrate divine worship as true priests of the
New Testament....

---

7. St. Thomas Aquinas, *Summa theologiae*, 3, 73, 3.
8. St. Leo the Great, *Sermons*, 63, 7.

In virtue of their common sacred ordination and mission, all priests are bound together in an intimate brotherhood, which should naturally and freely manifest itself in mutual aid, spiritual as well as material, pastoral as well as personal, in meetings and in a community of life, of labor, and of charity....

Deacons

29. At a lower level of the hierarchy are deacons, upon whom hands are imposed "not unto the priesthood but unto a ministry of service."[9] For strengthened by sacramental grace, in communion with the bishop and his group of priests, they serve the People of God in the ministry of the liturgy, of the word, and of charity. It is the duty of the deacons, to the extent that they have been authorized by competent authority, to administer baptism solemnly, to be custodians and dispensers of the Eucharist, to assist at and bless marriages in the name of the Church, to bring Viaticum to the dying, to read the sacred Scriptures to the faithful, to instruct and exhort the people, to preside at the worship and prayer of the faithful, to administer sacramentals, and to officiate at funeral and burial services....

The Laity

The Council's definition of the laity such as to exclude religious may have caused some problem for lay religious, especially the faithful laybrothers who serve so well. But it seemed necessary, for the Council wanted to emphasize the "secular quality that is proper and special to laywomen and men." It is within the course of its consideration of the lay vocation that the Council speaks of the family. This is undoubtedly the most basic unit among the People of God, the home Church. Here the parents exercise their headship and

---

9. *Constitutions of the Egyptian Church*, 3, 2.

form the Church of tomorrow. It is extremely important that this sense of the home Church be renewed. There is little hope that young people will grow into the mind and heart of Christ if these attitudes are not formative of the culture of the home.

It is also important that the family realize their ecclesial role. Parents cannot content themselves with raising up children only for the future of their own family. They must have a sense of Church and raise up children for the Church. This is the only source of future priests and bishops, the essential leadership of a Eucharistic people. The vocation crisis begins in the homes where parents are not willing to raise a child for the Church. We cannot emphasize too strongly the need for parents to foster priestly vocations among their children, for without these we cannot continue as a Church that finds its source and center in the Eucharist. Priests need to constantly remind parents of this.

Although the chapter on the hierarchy is by far the longest chapter in the constitution, the one on the laity is the most powerful, and almost revolutionary in its proclamation of human dignity. It makes it clear that participation in the priestly, prophetic, and kingly office of the Son of God become man belongs as much to the layperson as to the hierarch, albeit in a different mode.

30. ...Everything which has been said so far concerning the People of God applies equally to the laity, religious, and clergy. But there are certain things which pertain in particular to the laity, both men and women, by reason of their situation and mission....

34. The term laity is here understood to mean all the faithful except those in holy orders and those in a religious state sanctioned by the Church. These faithful are by baptism made one body with Christ and are established in the People of God. They are in their own way made sharers in the priestly, prophetic, and kingly function of Christ. They carry out their own part in the mission

of the whole Christian people with respect to the Church and the world.

A secular quality is proper and special to laypersons.... The laity, by their very vocation, seek the Kingdom of God by engaging in temporal affairs and by ordering them according to the plan of God. They live in the world, that is, in each and in all of the secular professions and occupations. They live in the ordinary circumstances of family and social life, from which the very web of their existence is woven. They are called there by God so that by exercising their proper function and being led by the spirit of the Gospel they can work for the sanctification of the world from within in the manner of leaven. In this way they can make Christ known to others, especially by the testimony of a life resplendent in faith, hope, and charity....

32. ...The chosen People of God are one: "one Lord, one faith, one baptism" (Eph. 4:5). As members they share a common dignity from their rebirth in Christ. They have the same filial grace and the same vocation to perfection. They possess in common one salvation, one hope, and one undivided charity. Hence, there is in Christ and in the Church no inequality on the basis of race or nationality, social condition or sex....

If therefore everyone in the Church does not proceed by the same path, nevertheless all are called to sanctity and have received an equal privilege of faith through the justice of God (cf. 2 Pet. 1:1). And if by the will of Christ some are made teachers, dispensers of mysteries, and shepherds on behalf of others, yet all share a true equality with regard to the dignity and to the activity common to all the faithful for the building up of the Body of Christ.

For the distinction which the Lord made between sacred ministers and the rest of the People of God entails a unifying purpose, since pastors and the other faithful are bound to each other by a mutual need. Pastors of the Church, following the example of the Lord, should minister to one another and to the other faithful. The faithful in their turn should enthusiastically lend their cooperative assistance to their pastors and teachers....

The Lay Apostolate

33. ... The lay apostolate is a participation in the saving mission of the Church. Through their baptism and confirmation all are commissioned to that apostolate by the Lord himself. Moreover, through the sacraments, especially the Holy Eucharist, there is communicated and nourished that charity toward God and fellow humans which is the soul of the entire apostolate. Now the laity are called in a special way to make the Church present and operative in those places and circumstances where only through them can it become the salt of the earth. Thus every layperson, by virtue of the very gifts bestowed upon him or her, is at the same time a witness and a living instrument of the mission of the Church "according to the measure of Christ's bestowal" (Eph. 4:7)....

Consequently let every opportunity be given to the laity so that, according to their abilities and the needs of the times, they may zealously participate in the saving work of the Church....

34. Besides intimately associating them with his life and his mission, Christ also gives them a share in his priestly function of offering spiritual worship for the glory of God and the salvation of all. For this reason the laity, dedicated to Christ and anointed by Holy Spirit, are marvelously called and equipped to produce in themselves ever more abundant fruits of the Spirit. For all their works, prayers, and apostolic endeavors, their married and family life, their daily labor, their mental and physical relaxation, if carried out in the Spirit, and even the hardships of life, if patiently borne — all of these become spiritual sacrifices acceptable to God through Jesus Christ (cf. 1 Pet. 2:5). During the celebration of the Eucharist, their sacrifices are most lovingly offered to the Father along with the Lord's body. Thus, as worshipers whose every deed is holy, the laity consecrate the world itself to God.

The Apostolic Mission of the Laity

35. Christ, the great Prophet, who proclaimed the Kingdom of his Father by the testimony of his life and the power of his words,

continually fulfills his prophetic office until his full glory is revealed. He does this not only through the hierarchy who teach in his name and with his authority but also through the laity. For that very purpose he made them his witnesses and gave them understanding of the faith and the grace of speech (cf. Acts 2:17–18; Rev. 19:10) so that the power of the Gospel might shine forth in their daily social and family life....

Let them not, then, hide this hope in the depths of their hearts, but even in the framework of secular life let them express it.... Husband and wife find their vocation in being to one another and to their children witnesses of faith in Christ and of love for him. The Christian family loudly proclaims both the present virtues of the Kingdom of God and the whole of a blessed life to come....

Some of them do all they can to provide sacred services when sacred ministers are lacking or are blocked by a persecuting regime. Many devote themselves entirely to apostolic work. But all ought to cooperate in the preaching and intensifying of the Kingdom of Christ in the world....

36. The faithful ought to learn the deepest meaning and value of all creation and how to relate it to the praise of God.... For while it must be recognized that the temporal sphere is governed by its own principles since it is properly concerned with the interests of this world, that ominous doctrine must rightly be rejected which attempts to build a society with no regard whatever for religion and which attacks and destroys the religious liberty of its citizens.

37. The laity have the right, as do all Christians, to receive in abundance from their pastors the spiritual benefits of the Church, especially the assistance of the Word of God and the sacraments. ...An individual layperson, by reason of the knowledge, compassion, or outstanding ability which he or she may enjoy, is permitted and sometimes is even required to express opinions in things which concern the good of the Church.... Let pastors recognize and promote the dignity as well as the responsibility of laypersons in the Church. Let them make use of their prudent advice. Let them confidently assign duties to them in the service of the Church, allowing them freedom and room for action. Further, let them encourage

laypersons so that they may undertake tasks on their own initiative. Attentively in Christ, let them consider with paternal love the projects, suggestions, and desires proposed by the laity. Furthermore let pastors respectfully acknowledge that just freedom which belongs to everyone in this earthly city.

A great many benefits are to be hoped for from this open dialogue between the laity and their pastors: in the laity, a strengthened sense of personal responsibility, a renewed enthusiasm, a more ready application of their talents to the projects of their pastors. The latter, for their part, aided by the experience of the laity, can more clearly and more suitably come to decisions regarding spiritual and temporal matters. In this way the whole Church strengthened by each one of it members can more effectively fulfill its mission for the life of the world.

38. Each individual layperson ought to stand before the world as a witness to the resurrection and life of the Lord Jesus and as a sign that God lives. As a body and individually the laity must do their part to nourish the world with spiritual fruits (cf. Gal. 5:22) and to spread abroad in it that spirit by which are animated those poor, meek, and peacemaking whom the Lord in the Gospel calls blessed (cf. Mt. 5:3–9). In a word, "what the soul is to the body, let Christians be to the world."[10]

The Call of the Whole Church to Holiness

The call of each and every member of the People of God to holiness which this document strongly reaffirms, should be most obvious. But the problem comes from the stuff we hang around the word "holiness." This word has so much baggage around it I wish we could throw it out and start all over with a new word: Holiness is heroic, it is odd, it is levitation and ecstasy, it is all that sort of stuff that just doesn't fit into an ordinary everyday life. Or so most have come to think from the admiring stories we have been fed about the saints of

10. *Letter to Diognetus*, 6.

old. Even a Mother Teresa seems rather ethereal, belonging
to a state unattainable to most of us. We have canonized too
many religious and too few laypersons. The Council tries to
cut through all of this:

> ... all the faithful of Christ of whatever rank or status are called to
> the fullness of the Christian life and to the perfection of charity. By
> this holiness a more human way of life is promoted even in the
> earthly society. (40)

Even here I have a difficulty. That word "perfection." How
often has that Gospel text been quoted out of context: "Be
perfect as your heavenly Father is perfect. . . . " What does the
Lord go on to say? " . . . who lets his rain fall upon the good
and bad alike, lets his sun shine on the just and the unjust."
Herein is God's perfection: compassionate love. There is here
no idea of some ethereal, moralistic, abstract "perfection." It
is simply living compassionate love, to love even those who
do not deserve to be loved. Or as Jesus said on another occasion: "Do good to those who hate you." Sure, this is heroic
in a way, but it is something that, with the help of God, we
can all do. And the constitution underlines some of the ways
in which we can effectively draw on that divine help, most
especially through participation in the sacramental life of the
Church.

39. Faith teaches that the Church, whose mystery is being set
forth by the Synod, is holy in a way which can never fail. For Christ,
the Son of God, who with the Father and the Spirit is praised as being "alone holy,"[11] loved the Church as his Bride, delivering himself
up for her. This he did that he might sanctify it (cf. Eph. 5:25–26).
He united it to himself as his own body and crowned it with the gift
of Holy Spirit for God's glory. Therefore in the Church everyone belonging to the hierarchy or being cared for by it is called to holiness

---

11. Roman Missal, *Gloria in excelsis*.

according to the saying of the Apostle: "For this is the will of God, your sanctification (cf. 1 Th. 4:3; cf. Eph. 1:4).

41. In the various types and duties of life, one and the same holiness is cultivated by all who are moved by the Spirit of God and who obey the voice of the Father, worshiping God the Father in spirit and truth. These follow the poor Christ, the humble and cross-bearing Christ, in order to be made worthy of being partakers in his glory. Every person should walk unhesitatingly according to his or her own personal gifts and duties in the path of a living faith which arouses hope and works through charity....

Laborers, whose work is often toilsome, should by their human exertions try to perfect themselves, aid their fellow citizens, and raise all of society and even creation itself to a better mode of existence. By their lively charity, joyful hope, and sharing one another's burdens, let them also truly imitate Christ, who roughened his hands with carpenter's tools and who in union with his Father is always at work for the salvation of women and men. By their daily work laborers can achieve greater apostolic sanctity.

Those who are oppressed by poverty, infirmity, sickness, or various other hardships, as well as those who suffer persecution for justice' sake — may they all know that in a special way they are united with the suffering Christ for the salvation of the world. The Lord called them blessed in his Gospel....

All of Christ's faithful, therefore, whatever be the condition, duties, and circumstances of their lives, will grow in holiness day by day through these very situations if they accept all of them with faith from the hand of their heavenly Father and if they cooperate with the divine will by showing every one through their earthly activities the love with which God has loved the world....

Religious

Holiness is being a loving and compassionate person. The constitution points out that each does this according to his or her personal gifts and duties: the bishop by his care and service; married couples by faithful love, sustaining one another; the single by his or her good example; the laborer at daily work. Religious, then, are not all that special. But they have taken a public stand that this is what their lives are about, a wholehearted dedication to God and to their fellows in love. They bind themselves to do this by vows or something like vows — promises, oaths. And they form communities to support each other in doing this. It is a good way to live among the pilgrim People of God, which, as the constitution reminds us in one of its more noteworthy statements, was "established by Christ as a fellowship of life, charity, and truth."

Life according to the Evangelical Councils

43. The evangelical counsels of chastity dedicated to God, poverty, and obedience are based upon the words and example of the Lord. They were further commended by the Apostles and the Fathers and other teachers and shepherds of the Church. The counsels are a divine gift, which the Church has received from its Lord and which it ever preserves with the help of his grace. Church authority has the duty under the inspiration of Holy Spirit of interpreting these evangelical counsels, of regulating their practice, and finally of establishing stable forms of living according to them.

Thus it has come about that various forms of solitary and community life, as well as different religious families have grown up. Advancing the progress of their members and the welfare of the whole body of Christ, these groups have been like branches sprouting out wondrously and abundantly from a tree growing in the field of the Lord from a seed divinely planted.

These religious families give their members the support of greater stability in their way of life, a proven method of acquiring perfection, familial association in the militia of Christ, and liberty strengthened by obedience. Thus these religious can securely fulfill and faithfully observe their religious profession and rejoicing in spirit make progress on the road of charity.

From the point of view of the divine and hierarchical structure of the Church, the religious state of life is not an intermediate one between the clerical and lay states. Rather the faithful of Christ are called by God from both these latter states of life so that they may enjoy this particular gift in the life of the Church and thus each in his or her own way forward the saving mission of the Church.

44. The faithful of Christ can bind themselves to the three counsels either by vows or by other sacred bonds which are like vows in their purpose. Through such a bond a person is totally dedicated to God by an act of supreme love and is committed to the honor and service of God under a new and special title.

It is true that through baptism each has died to sin and has been consecrated to God. However, in order to derive more abundant fruit from this baptismal grace, religious intend by the profession of the evangelical counsels in the Church to free themselves from those obstacles which might draw them away from the fervor of charity and the perfection of divine worship. Thus they are more intimately consecrated to divine service. This consecration gains in perfection since by virtue of firmer and steadier bonds it serves as a better symbol of the unbreakable link between Christ and his Spouse, the Church.

By the charity to which they lead, the evangelical counsels join their followers to the Church and its mystery in a special way. Since this is so, the spiritual life of these followers should be devoted to the welfare of the whole Church. Thence arises their duty of working to implant and strengthen the Kingdom of Christ in souls and to extend that Kingdom in every land. This duty is to be discharged to the extent of their capacities and in keeping with the form of their proper vocation. The chosen means may be prayer or active undertakings. It is for this reason the Church preserves and fosters the special character of its various religious communities.

Although the religious state constituted by the profession of the evangelical counsels does not belong to the hierarchical structure of the Church, nevertheless it belongs inseparably to its life and holiness....

The Place of Religious in the Institutional Church

45. ... Any institute of perfection and its individual members can be removed from the jurisdiction of the local Ordinaries by the Supreme Pontiff and subjected to himself alone. This is possible by virtue of his primacy over the entire Church. He does so in order to provide more adequately for the necessities of the entire flock of the Lord and in consideration of the common good....

By its approval the Church not only raises the religious profession to the dignity of a canonical state. By its liturgical action it also manifests that it is a state consecrated to God. The Church, by the authority given it by God, accepts the vows of those making profession; with public prayer it implores aid and grace from God for them. It commends them to God, imparts a spiritual blessing on them, and accompanies their self-offering with the Eucharistic Sacrifice.

46. ... Finally, everyone should realize that the profession of the evangelical counsels, though entailing the renunciation of certain values which undoubtedly merit high esteem, does not detract from a genuine development of the human person. Rather by its very nature it is most beneficial to that development. For the counsels, voluntarily undertaken according to each one's personal vocation, contribute greatly to purification of heart and spiritual liberty. They continually enkindle the fervor of charity. As the example of so many saintly founders shows, the counsels are especially able to pattern the Christian person after the manner of the virginal and humble life which Christ the Lord elected for himself and which his Virgin Mother also chose.

Let no one think that by their consecration religious have become strangers to their fellows or useless citizens of this earthly city. For even though in some instances religious do not directly mingle with their contemporaries, yet in a more profound sense these same religious are united with them in the heart of Christ and cooperate with them spiritually so that the work of building up the earthly city can always have its foundation in the Lord and can tend toward him lest perhaps those who build this city will have labored in vain.

The Eschatological Nature
of the Pilgrim Church

The People of God are a people on the move. We are going someplace. But we are not just stumbling along, with some vague goal. Life takes on quite a different perspective when we are able to project ourselves into our goal and then work from that vantage point. When we take a stand and make a declaration — I am a disciple of Christ who is going to follow him all the way — it opens up the space precisely for us to do that — no matter what the past has been. So St. Paul says: "Forgetting what is behind, press forward to the mark." This is the eschatological nature of the Pilgrim Church. "Eschatological" may be a big word, but what it is saying is: we are really in touch with where we are going — thanks to the communion of saints — and this empowers all that we do as a People on route.

48. The Church, to which we are all called in Christ Jesus and in which we acquire sanctity through the grace of God, will attain its full perfection only in the glory of heaven. Then will come the time of the restoration of all things (Acts 3:21). Then the human race as well as the entire world, which is intimately related to humans and achieves its purpose through them, will be perfectly re-established in Christ (cf. Eph. 1:10; Col. 1:20; 2 Pet. 3:10–13)....

The promised restoration which we are awaiting has already begun in Christ, is carried forward in the mission of Holy Spirit, and through her continues in the Church....However, until there is a new heaven and a new earth where justice dwells (cf. 2 Pet. 3:13), the pilgrim Church in its sacraments and institutions, which pertain to this present time, takes on the appearances of this passing world. It dwells among creatures who groan and travail in pain until now and await the revelation of the daughters and sons of God (cf. Rom. 8:19–22)....

Since we know not the day nor the hour, on our Lord's advice we must constantly stand guard. Thus when we have finished the one and only course of our earthly life (cf. Heb. 9:27) we may merit to enter into the marriage feast with him and to be numbered among the blessed (cf. Mt. 25:31–46).

We Remain One with Those
Who Have Gone Before

49. ...All who belong to Christ, having his Spirit, form one Church and cleave together in him (cf. Eph. 4:16). Therefore the union of the wayfarers with the brothers and sisters who have gone to sleep in the peace of Christ is not in the least interrupted. On the contrary, according to the perennial faith of the Church, it is strengthened through the exchanging of spiritual goods. For by reason of the fact that those in heaven are more closely united with Christ, they establish the whole Church more firmly in holiness, lend nobility to the worship which the Church offers on earth to God, and in many ways contribute to its great upbuilding (cf. 1 Cor. 12:12–27). For after they have been received into their heavenly home and are present to the Lord (cf. 2 Cor. 5:8) through him and with him and in him they do not cease to intercede with the Father for us....

50. ...By its very nature every genuine testimony of love which we show to those in heaven tends toward and terminates in Christ, who is the "crown of the saints."[12] Through him it tends toward and terminates in God, who is wonderful in his saints and is magnified in them....The authentic cult of the saints consists not so much in the multiplying of external acts but rather in the intensity of our active love. By such love for our own greater good and that of the Church we seek from the saints "example in their way of life, fellowship in their communion, and aid by their intercession."[13]

---

12. Roman Breviary, Invitatory Antiphon, Feast of All Saints.
13. From the Preface granted for use in various dioceses.

The Role of the Blessed Virgin Mary, Mother of God in the Mystery of Christ and the Church

This Dogmatic Constitution concerning Church actually contains another constitution within it. Whether it should have or not will continue to be debated. Ecumenical sensitivities argued in many directions, as did Marian piety. Chapter VIII with its own five "chapters" does seek to place Mary, the mother of Jesus, in her proper context among the People of God. She is so unique this is not easy to do. Moreover, she is our mother, and it is difficult to keep things fully in perspective when one speaks about one's mother. The chapter is concise, a good bit shorter than the chapter on the bishops. On the whole, I think one reading it finds it a beautiful and enriching piece that is ecumenically sensitive and yet gives Mary all the honor that is due her in a most balanced way.

52. Wishing in his supreme goodness and wisdom to effect the redemption of the world, "when the fullness of time came, God sent his Son, born of a woman...that we might receive the adoption of sons and daughters" (Gal. 4:4–5). "He for us and for our salvation came down from heaven and was incarnate by Holy Spirit from the Virgin Mary."[14] This divine mystery of salvation is revealed to us and continued in the Church which the Lord established as his own body. In this Church, adhering to Christ the Head and having communion with all his saints, the faithful must also venerate the memory "above all of the glorious and perpetual Virgin Mary, Mother of our God and Lord Jesus Christ."[15]

Mary's Role in Salvation History

53. At the message of the angel, the Virgin Mary received the Word of God in her heart and in her body and gave Life to the

---

14. *The Constantinopolitan Creed.*
15. First Canon of the Roman Missal.

world. Hence she is acknowledged and honored as being truly the Mother of God and Mother of the Redeemer. Redeemed in an especially sublime manner by reason of the merits of her Son and united to him by a close and indissoluble bond, she is endowed with the supreme office and dignity of being the Mother of the Son of God. As a result she is also the favorite daughter of the Father and the temple of Holy Spirit. Because of this gift of sublime grace she far surpasses all other creatures both in heaven and on earth.

At the same time, however, because she belongs to the offspring of Adam she is one with all human beings in their need for salvation. Indeed she is "clearly the mother of the members of Christ...since she cooperated out of love so that there might be born in the Church the faithful who are members of Christ their Head."[16] Therefore she is also hailed as a pre-eminent and altogether singular member of the Church and as the Church's model and excellent exemplar in faith and charity. Taught by Holy Spirit the Catholic Church honors her with filial affection and piety as a most beloved mother....

56. The Father of mercies willed that the consent of the predestined mother should precede the Incarnation so that just as a woman contributed to death, so also a woman should contribute to life....

57. The union of the Mother with the Son in the work of salvation was manifested from the time of Christ's virginal conception up to his death....

58. Thus the Blessed Virgin advanced in her pilgrimage of faith and loyally persevered in her union with her Son unto the cross. There she stood in keeping with the divine plan (cf. Jn. 19:25), suffering grievously with her only-begotten Son. There she united herself with a maternal heart to his sacrifice and lovingly consented to the immolation of this Victim which she herself had brought forth. Christ Jesus dying on the cross gave her as mother to his disciple. This he did when he said: "Woman, behold your son" (Jn. 19:26–27)....

59. Finally, preserved free from all guilt of original sin, the Immaculate Virgin was taken up body and soul into heavenly glory upon

---

16. St. Augustine, *Concerning Holy Virginity*, 6.

the completion of her earthly sojourn. She was exalted by the Lord
as Queen of all in order that she might be the more thoroughly
conformed to her Son, the Lord of lords (cf. Rev. 19:16) and the
conqueror of sin and death.

Mary's Place among the People of God

60. We have but one Mediator, as we know from the words of
the Apostle: "For there is one God and one Mediator between God
and humans, himself a man, Christ Jesus, who gave himself a ransom
for all" (1 Tim. 2:5–6). The maternal duty of Mary toward women
and men in no way obscures or diminishes the unique mediation
of Christ but rather shows its power. For all the saving influences
of the Blessed Virgin on women and men originate not from some
inner necessity but from the divine pleasure. They flow forth from
the superabundance of the merits of Christ, rest on his mediation,
depend entirely on it, and draw all their power from it. In no way do
they impede the immediate union of the faithful with Christ. Rather
they foster this union....

66. Especially after the Council of Ephesus the cult of the People
of God toward Mary wonderfully increased in veneration and love,
in invocation and imitation, according to her own prophetic words:
"All generations shall call me blessed; because he who is mighty has
done great things for me" (Lk. 1:48). As it has always existed in the
Church, this cult is altogether special. Still it differs essentially from
the cult of adoration which is offered to the Incarnate Word, as well
as to the Father and Holy Spirit....

67. ...This Synod earnestly exhorts theologians and preachers
of the divine word that in treating of the unique dignity of the
Mother of God they carefully and equally avoid the falsity of exag-
geration on the one hand and the excess of narrow-mindedness on
the other. Pursuing the study of sacred Scripture, the holy Fathers,
the doctors, and the liturgies of the Church and under the guidance
of the Church's teaching authority let them rightly explain the offices and privileges of the Blessed Virgin which are always related to
Christ, the source of all truth, sanctity, and piety....

69. Let the entire body of the faithful pour forth persevering prayer to the Mother of God and Mother of men and women. Let them implore that she who aided the beginnings of the Church by her prayers may now, exalted as she is in heaven above all the saints and angels, intercede with her Son in the fellowship of all the saints. May she do so until all the peoples of the human family, whether they are honored with the name of Christian or whether they still do not know their Savior, are happily gathered together in peace and harmony into the one People of God for the glory of the Most Holy and Undivided Trinity.

The funerals of two holy men characterize in a way the shift that was taking place within the Church as this constitution was elaborated. The one took place a few months before the promulgation of the constitution; the other was that of the pope who promulgated it. Pope John XXIII was waked in true pontifical style, laid out under the baldachino over the tomb of St. Peter in full papal regalia. Only a chosen few, tickets in hand, were admitted to the basilica for the final obsequies. Long before his funeral, Paul VI's tiara had been disposed of to raise money for the poor. The simple wooden casket lay on the ground in front of the basilica. And all the People of God were welcomed into the embrace of Bernini's colonnade to join in the prayer for the departed. Atop the simple coffin there was an open Bible and as the obsequies progressed, the Spirit blew the pages this way and that; the whole of the Scriptures were open to the People.

We are the People of God, each with his or her own particular role of collegial leadership. If we spend some time with this constitution we can come to a clearer vision of our goal as individuals and as a People, a very special People: "a chosen race, a royal priesthood, a holy nation, a purchased people." If we listen attentively to what this constitution tells us about the role of the Spirit in our lives as individuals and as a People, we can move confidently forward, drawing ever closer to all our brothers and sisters in compassionate love.

We are the People of God.

2

The Corollaries

DECREE CONCERNING
EASTERN CATHOLIC CHURCHES

The People of God, and their shepherds who gathered at the Second Vatican Council, are a richly hued People. They come from East and West, North and South. They wear all different kinds of clothes, eat different kinds of food, speak different languages. They have all sorts of customs, celebrate different kinds of liturgies, and look to different traditions — but within the one Christian Tradition. For we are the one People of God. The shepherds were meeting at Rome, under the presidency of the Bishop of Rome, the Patriarch of the West. Some of the brothers from the East were there, but not many. Some of the Eastern brothers had been restrained from coming by repressive governments. Others were held back by age-old separations and anathemas, which happily were soon to be lifted. Some few stood in a tribune on the side as observers.

The fathers of the Council wanted to be sure all knew that the Church embraced brothers and sisters of East and West. More, the brothers from the West wanted to bow deferen-

tially to their brothers and sisters from the East, to whom
they owed so much. It may be only an accident of history —
though the eyes of faith would always see the workings of
an all-provident Lord behind it — that the primacy came
to Rome. But one can never forget that Peter first preached
in Jerusalem, first sat in Antioch. Thus the Council fathers
spoke a word concerning the Christians of the East in the
Decree concerning Eastern Catholic Churches:

The Catholic Church holds in high esteem the institutions of the
Eastern Churches, their liturgical rites, ecclesiastical traditions and
Christian way of life. For distinguished as they are by their venerable antiquity, they are illumined by the Tradition which was handed
down from the apostles through the Fathers and which forms part
of the divinely revealed and undivided heritage of the universal
Church. (1)

Like all the other decrees this document contains a number of practical provisions, which are meant to set things
in motion, to get the Church, and more especially the bureaucracy within the Church, moving in new and renewing
directions. The fathers wanted to preserve and foster the rich
variety of rites alive among the People of God. Rite means
much more than just liturgical rites and formulas; it includes
"liturgy, ecclesiastical discipline, and spiritual heritage." As
usual the Council sought to teach by example as well as
by word and frequently opened its working sessions with a
celebration of the liturgy following one of the ancient Eastern rites. The Eastern Patriarchs were given due precedence
in the Council. Fathers from the Eastern Churches, though
they were relatively few in number, were included in virtually every important commission. They were welcomed to
speak freely and regularly in the Council debates. They made
a vital contribution to another corollary to the Dogmatic
Constitution concerning Church, the Decree concerning Ecu-

menism, which speaks on "the special position of the Eastern Churches" and gives them significant consideration in its determinations.

This Decree concerning Eastern Catholic Churches in itself has very great ecumenical import. Its concluding statement reads as follows:

This Synod feels great joy in the fruitful and zealous collaboration between the Eastern and Western Catholic Churches and at the same time declares that all these directives of law are laid down in view of the present situation until such time as the Catholic Church and the separated Eastern Churches come together into complete unity. (30)

This tells our fellow Christians in the Eastern Churches that we do not see the Eastern Catholic Churches as substitutes for them in the communion of the whole Church but rather as lines thrown out, bridges being built, with the hope that true and full unity will soon follow. Yet unfortunately there are things in the decree at which our separated brothers and sisters can take offense, especially the unilateral allowance for sharing in sacraments and other things sacred:

27. ... Eastern Christians who are separated in good faith from the Catholic Church, if they ask of their own accord and have the right dispositions, may be granted the sacraments of penance, the Eucharist, and the anointing of the sick. Furthermore Catholics may ask for these same sacraments from those non-Catholic ministers whose Churches possess valid sacraments as often as necessity or a genuine spiritual benefit recommends such a course of action and when access to a Catholic priest is physically or morally impossible.

28. Again, in view of these very same principles Catholics may for a just cause join with their separated Eastern sisters and brothers in sacred functions, things, and places....

This decree also bypasses the fact that our Orthodox brothers and sisters see the differences in rite, which are celebrated here, as actually expressing or at least reflecting theological differences. These are, of course, matters that must be the subject of serious ecumenical dialogue, which is precisely what the Decree concerning Ecumenism seeks to foster.

DECREE CONCERNING ECUMENISM

The ecumenical movement is far from dead. It is, indeed, living in ways far beyond what the Council envisioned — and perhaps in ways that the Council fathers feared. The high-level meetings and dialogues no longer get the press they did at first. They have, thank God, become so much a part of the ongoing activity of the Churches, like the pope's visits to countries around the world, that they hardly command press coverage. Yet they go on. True, they have their hotter and their cooler moments as different hierarchs and leaders succeed one another in the different Churches. And there are still segments of Christianity that rather than responding to the Catholic Church's overtures have only renewed their attacks upon this Church. These, thank God, are very much in the minority on the overall world scene, though their presence can be acutely felt in particular locales.

The decree has stressed, and rightly, that true rapprochement can take place only through honest dialogue. The richness that lies ahead for us and has already been somewhat experienced is found in each of us bringing to the other the fullness of who we are, of what we have received from God, of all that has developed to the good within our particular Church during the years of separation. Glossing over things may be a certain sort of irenicism that feels good and could even in some way smooth the path for true ecumenism, but it is not true ecumenism; the Council fathers feared this. Hence the insistence on formal and well-regulated meetings by truly competent women and men. For the most part this is what has taken place on the institutional level. But the popular level has run far ahead of this. The decree had allowed for worshiping together in a controlled way, the purposes clearly in mind and the hierarchy making the prudent decisions:

As for common worship, it may not be regarded as a means to be used indiscriminately for the restoration of unity among Christians. Such worship depends chiefly on two principles: it should signify the unity of the Church and it should provide a sharing in the means of grace. The fact that it should signify unity generally rules out common worship. Yet the gaining of a needed grace sometimes commends it.

The practical course to be adopted, after due regard has been given to all the circumstances of time, place, and persons, is left to the prudent decision of the local episcopal authority.... (8)

But the laity have taken the matter in their own hands. Where once a Catholic piously asked the pastor's permission to attend a funeral or wedding in a Protestant Church, today Catholics feel free to attend any service in any Christian Church, and some even feel free to share in the Communion offered. And Protestants and other Christians for the most part know themselves welcome at Catholic services, though they still sense some reservations on the part of Catholics to share the Eucharist and the other sacraments.

The result of this has been a watering down in the popular mind of the differences in teaching among the different Christian Churches, a sense that this difference in doctrinal teaching does not really matter. In the face of the great challenges that confront all Christians in an increasingly materialistic and hedonistic world, these differences seem little and quite theoretical, at least to the many Christians who have had relatively little theological education. It is at the level of practical moral teachings that immediately touch the daily lives of the average Christian that differences are most keenly felt.

The Council fathers had suggested that "the ecumenical dialogue could start with discussions concerning the application of the Gospel to moral questions" (23). Some have thought this would have been disastrous and are grateful that this suggestion was not followed. But in fact it might have been good, and it is not too late for such discussion to begin in earnest. Perhaps Pope John Paul II's recent encyclical on morality[1] will open the way for this. In dealing with these issues, which touch us most intimately, we are forced back to the deeper questions: What is the teaching authority of my Church? Where does it come from? Is there an infallible guidance somewhere within the Christian Church? What is the principle of unity in teaching? What is the role of the conscience of the individual Christian? What is the connection between celebrating Eucharist together and standing together on moral questions? ...

Perhaps today the dialogical attitude inculcated by this decree is more needed within the individual Churches and in the Christian's response to the human community, at least in respect to these moral issues. Christians of all denominations need to approach with love, reverence, and respect all those who differ from them, to listen to them, and to be willing to pray with them. "By this shall all know you are my disciples, that you have love...." "See how these Christians love...."

One of the striking elements of this Decree concerning Ecumenism is the humble avowal on the part of the Council fathers that the sin of a disunited Christianity finds its cause in all of us. We all stand in need of a change of heart. We are

---

1. Pope John Paul II, *Veritatis splendor,* August 6, 1993.

all a pilgrim People of God going together toward Christ. It is a common journey. No longer do we stand still and demand that others journey toward Rome. We have all been baptized into the one Christ. We already have a oneness beyond anything we can actually conceive. In a growing awareness of this oneness we are called to action: to live who we are. It is not a question of becoming friends and forgetting about the claims of truth. It is not either/or. It is being friends enough to be able to speak the truth to each other in love and together to seek the fullness of Truth, our common Lord, Jesus Christ.

The Decree concerning Ecumenism represents for the Roman Church an immense conversion and renewal. It flows out of the renewed realization of Church as People of God and a renewed turning to the source of our Christian life, to those truths set forth in the two dogmatic constitutions of the Council. For the fathers the insight expressed in these documents not only demanded a conversion on the part of every Catholic but was also a call to action. The fathers in no way watered down the Catholic Church's sense of itself:

It is through the Catholic Church alone, which is the all-embracing means of salvation, that the fullness of the means of salvation can be obtained. It was to the apostolic college alone of which Peter is the head, that we believe our Lord entrusted all the blessing of the New Covenant in order to establish on earth the one Body of Christ into which all those should be fully incorporated who already belong in any way to God's People. (3)

Yet it had much to say about the renewed way the apostolic college and all the members of the Church should act, not only in the two constitutions and this decree but in other corollaries to them.

DECREE CONCERNING THE BISHOPS' PASTORAL OFFICE IN THE CHURCH

The Decree concerning the Bishops' Pastoral Office in the Church did repeat with a certain fullness some of the things found in the constitutions and other decrees, but it left other matters, such as ecumenical ministry, largely to the foregoing decree. Each decree is written so that to some extent it can stand on its own; hence the repetition. Yet all of them, and especially this one, flow from the Dogmatic Constitution concerning Church and seek to renew the Church so that it can fulfill its mission in the modern world.

One of the more beautiful sections of this decree is what might be called the description of the good shepherd, a section the bishops themselves can use as a constant inspiration or, if need be, examination of conscience:

In exercising his office of father and pastor, a bishop should stand in the midst of his people as one who serves. Let him be a good shepherd who knows his sheep and whose sheep know him. Let him be a true father who excels in the spirit of love and solicitude for all and to whose divinely conferred authority all gratefully submit themselves. Let him so gather and mold the whole family of his flock that all, conscious of their own duties, may live and work in the communion of love.

To accomplish those things effectively, a bishop "ready for every good work" (2 Tim. 2:21) and "enduring all things for the sake of the chosen ones" (2 Tim. 2:10), should arrange his life in such a way as to accommodate it to the needs of the time.

A bishop should always welcome priests with a special love since they assume in part the bishop's duties and cares and carry the weight of them day by day so zealously. He should regard his priests as sons and friends. By his readiness to listen to them and by his trusting familiarity, let him seek to promote the whole of pastoral work of the entire diocese.

He should concern himself about the spiritual, intellectual, and material condition of his priests so that they can live holy and devout lives and fulfill their ministry faithfully and fruitfully. For this reason, he should encourage institutes and set up special meetings in which the priests can gather at times for spiritual programs that will renew their lives and for study programs, especially in Scripture and theology, and for ones that will touch on the major social issues and new methods of pastoral ministry. With an effective mercy a bishop should care for priests who are in any sort of danger or who in some way have faltered.

In order to be able to better serve the faithful according to the particular situations they find themselves in, the bishop should strive to become duly acquainted with their needs in their social context, using the proper means, especially social research. He should manifest his concern for all, no matter what their age, condition, or nationality, be they natives, strangers, or foreigners. In exercising this pastoral care he should preserve for the faithful the share proper to them in Church affairs, acknowledging their duty and right to collaborate actively in building up the mystical Body of Christ.

He should deal lovingly with the separated brothers and sisters, urging the faithful also to conduct themselves with great kindness and charity in their regard and fostering ecumenism as it is understood by the Church. He should also have the welfare of the non-baptized at heart so that upon them too there may shine the charity of Christ Jesus to whom the bishop is a witness before all women and men.... (16)

The bishops especially wanted to treat of matters that deeply concerned them but that they did not want to give the dignity of a place in the Dogmatic Constitution concerning Church. One of these was the business of coadjutor bishops and auxiliaries, sometimes used by higher authority to circumscribe the local bishop and the replacement of these in large part by episcopal vicars, a newly developed role in the administration of dioceses. These concerns follow naturally from the question of diocesan boundaries. If a bishop needs many vicars, there is certainly a question as to whether he can in truth be a true pastor to the flock committed to him. Some creative thinking needs to be done as to how to keep dioceses small enough so that a bishop can truly know his flock and yet not unduly multiply all the structures that usually go with a diocese. Can not a cluster of small dioceses share certain bureaus and services, such as tribunals, without undermining the true pastoral role of the local bishop?

Perhaps the sorest point with the bishops is the bureaucracy that surrounds the Roman Pontiff, lays claim to his full authority, and makes all sorts of demands on the local bishops, profoundly affecting the exercise of their pastoral office. The decree recognizes the authority of these curial offices but "strongly desires" that these be reorganized and better adapted to the times, especially these times when the true collegiality of the bishops is being recognized. The Council fathers want the makeup of these offices to be much more international. And they want diocesan bishops to be made members so the pope is more fully and directly informed about what is actually transpiring on the local pastoral scene. And they want qualified laypersons to be involved, too.

Along the same lines the fathers asked that the office of papal legates be more precisely defined.

The decree also brought into existence or fostered the development of bodies to express the collegiality of the bishops. There would be a synod of bishops, meeting regularly to advise the pope on issues of the day. And there would be national or regional conferences of bishops. The bishops themselves were timid about giving any of their authority to these conferences. The Holy See was even more loath to share authority with them. In the end the conferences got very little true authority, precisely that which the Holy See wants to give them. And even that is to be closely supervised.

What is most interesting is perhaps what is not found

in this decree nor in the Dogmatic Constitution concerning Church. Little or nothing is said about how bishops are to be chosen. As one archbishop noted: I have been a bishop for twenty-seven years and I still do not know how bishops are named. It is surprising that the Council fathers did not address themselves to this crucial question. But then perhaps the very ones who hold the power in this sphere held the power in the Council to keep the question off the agenda. It is difficult to see though how a man can be expected to fulfill all the roles he is asked to in regard to a diocese, its clergy, and laypeople when he comes in as a complete stranger, perhaps even from another part of the country or world where customs and culture are very different. It will take him years; in fact he can never hope to establish the kind of rapport with the presbyterate that a man would have who lived, labored, and loved in the diocese all his priestly life, who truly knows the priests as brothers, and who is thoroughly imbued with the customs and culture of the place. It is his culture. On the other hand what does it say to the priests of a diocese when their superiors seem to be saying that there is not a single man among them who is good enough to be promoted to the leadership role; an outsider has to brought in. One would think that these men, whom the Council fathers want to work so closely with their bishops, should have some say in the selection of their leader.

DECREE CONCERNING THE MINISTRY AND LIFE OF PRIESTS

In its opening lines and in its closing the Decree concerning the Ministry and Life of Priests indicates that the bishops at Council have some sense of the tensions under which priests labor: They are drawn apart from the world and are yet to be in it among the people. They need to have a deep knowledge of the Gospel with its divine wisdom and truth. And they need to have a deep knowledge of the world and the human wisdom necessary to apply the Gospel to today's rapidly evolving society. They are to be community formers and leaders with a world vision, and yet they are to conform completely to the will of the bishop. In fact the decree goes so far as to say the priest is required to accept and carry out not only whatever is commanded but even whatever is recommended by the pope, bishop, and other superiors. This goes beyond the demands of any vow of obedience.

When the fathers tell priests to be grateful for everything they receive to live a decent life and go on to invite them to embrace voluntary poverty, one racks one's brain for something similar in the decree the bishops wrote for themselves. When one hears the priest told he should have the kind of dwelling that no one will fear to visit, even the humblest, one cannot help but think of cardinalatial mansions and episcopal palaces that even priests are afraid to approach.

Here, as in the Dogmatic Constitution concerning Church, with the new understanding of episcopal orders it is strongly emphasized that the participation in the priesthood of Christ that is enjoyed and exercised by the ministerial priest is a secondary participation, wholly derivative from that of the bishop. What is not brought out is that this does not make the priest a second-class person or member of Christ. While the priesthood the man exercises is of a second order and derivative — a diversity of ministry but oneness of mission, as the Decree concerning the Apostolate of the Laity aptly expresses it — as members of Christ and of his Church, priest and bishop are equals. This is a distinction that is perhaps not fully worked out in the Council documents nor even in the theology of Church and sacrament that has developed since the Council. It certainly is difficult to maintain in practice. But it is essential that it be maintained if Church — bishops, beginning with the Bishop of Rome, priests, and laity — are going to give priests the respect due them and priestly morale is going to flourish, which is essential for the fostering of priestly vocations. The consequences of an all-too-common failure to do this are painfully evident in the Church today: low morale among the priests, many resignations, few vocations. This is a major issue the Roman Catholic Church has to face.

The Council fathers, all bishops and superiors, see priests too much in the context of the fulfillment of their own ministerial aspirations. The chapter on the ministry of priests is put before that on the life of priests. And in this latter chapter the bishops explicitly say that what they have to say to priests about their personal life they see in the context of the renewal of the Church, the spread of the Gospel, and the dialogue with the modern world. There seems little consideration for the priest himself as a person, no word about his freedom, his dignity, his taking any initiative, even though the decree does affirm that the Spirit is "impelling the Church to open new avenues of approach to the world today [and] is suggesting and fostering fitting adaptations in the ministry of priests" and it calls for the establishment of a priestly senate, which "will be able to give effective assistance to the bishop in his government of the diocese." It would have been well if the bishops had addressed to themselves in regard to their priests something like the good directives they give the priests in regard to the laity:

Priests [bishops] must sincerely acknowledge and promote the dignity of the laity [priests] and the role which is proper to them in the mission of the Church. They should scrupulously honor that just freedom which is due to everyone in this earthly city. They should listen to the laity [priests] willingly, consider their wishes in a fraternal spirit, and recognize their experience and competence in the different areas of human activity so that together with them they will be able to read the signs of the times.

While testing spirits to see if they be of God, priests [bishops] should discover with the instinct of faith, acknowledge with joy, and foster with diligence the various humble and exalted charisms of the laity [priests]. Among the other gifts of God which are found in abundance among the faithful [priests], those are worthy of special attention which are drawing many to a deeper spiritual life. Priests [bishops] should also confidently entrust to the laity [priests] duties in the service of the Church, allowing them freedom and room for action. In fact, on suitable occasions, they should invite them to undertake works on their own initiative. (9)

The Dogmatic Constitution concerning Church insisted that there is a difference not just of degree but of essence between the priesthood of the faithful and that of the one ordained to ministry. Yet neither there nor here is the precise nature of this difference spelled out with any theological depth. Nonetheless there is still a lot in the wording of this decree that says to the layperson that the priest is somehow better. What is worse, the comparative elements in the passages on celibacy imply that the married priest somehow doesn't quite make it, not to speak of the married layperson. In seeking to prove the reasonableness of demanding something of all Western priests, which as the fathers admit is "not demanded by the nature of the priesthood" (16), they go too far. Any vocation director would question the validity of the statement: "Perfect continence is never denied to those who ask" (16). In speaking of celibacy for the Kingdom the fathers might have done well to have said something about the joy of generativity a priest can experience in calling forth young men to follow him in the priesthood. This extensive treatment of a particular positive law of the Western Church, with little said about the married priest and his concerns and way to holiness, justifies again the claim of many of the Eastern hierarchs that the Council was in fact very much a Western synod rather than a truly catholic and ecumenical council.

The decree does say very beautifully:

The purpose which priests pursue by their ministry and life is the glory of God the Father as it is to be achieved in Christ. And that glory consists in this: that women and men knowingly, freely, and gratefully accept what God has achieved perfectly through Christ and manifest it in their whole lives. Hence, whether engaged in prayer and adoration, preaching the Word, offering the Eucharistic Sacrifice, ministering the other sacraments, or performing any of the works of the ministry for women and men, priests are contributing to the extension of God's glory as well as to the development of divine life in women and men. (2)

One of the very positive elements of this decree is the strong affirmation that it belongs to the office of pastor to form genuine Christian community with a community spirit that embraces not only the local Church but the universal Church as well, a community that finds its basis and center in the celebration of the most Holy Eucharist and is dedicated to various works of charity and mutual help, as well as to missionary activity and to different forms of Christian witness.

Laypersons might ponder on this decree to grow in compassion for their priests and perhaps learn to encourage and even challenge them a bit. But priests for the most part are not going to find in it an encouraging word.

DECREE CONCERNING PRIESTLY FORMATION

The Decree concerning Priestly Formation, the complement to the Decree concerning the Ministry and Life of Priests, is not an outstanding document either. There has been a veritable revolution in seminary training and formation, and the decree did its part to open the way for that within the current of the whole renewing force within the Church. However, in practice the renewal has been perhaps more in the training and education than in the formation of candidates for the priesthood. And this decree in a way is responsible for this. It has mandated such an immense amount of knowledge that the future priest is to acquire that, even though it called for clearing out irrelevant and specialized matters, it has left the poor student with little time for the formation of the mind and heart of Christ in the man who is to go forth to be Christ in the midst of his people, for the man whose life has to be filled with a personal love of Christ if his commitment to celibacy is not going to be an empty, sterile reality leading to deep loneliness.

Bishops hard pressed for priests are loath to allow any more years for priestly formation, yet the additional study load and the mandated pastoral experience cannot possibly fit in the old wine skin without the spaciousness necessary for personal evolution in the Spirit of Christ being totally sacrificed.

More courageous and visionary ordinaries have taken this into account. Dioceses in some countries have introduced a two-year program between philosophy and theology or between the completion of undergraduate studies and the four-year program geared specifically toward ministerial priesthood. The first of these two years is devoted almost entirely to personal development — human and spiritual or natural and supernatural or humane and Christic. During the second year, the candidate repeatedly goes forth for a few weeks and works in one or another of the apostolates of the diocese under a dedicated priest and then returns to the seminary to integrate his experience with the help of the guiding father there. In the course of the year the seminarian will have an opportunity to experience eight or ten of the various aspects of the local Church's ministry, integrate this dimension into his own growing sense of himself as a member of the presbyterate, of the diocese and have a very good sense of what he is seeking in his study of the Scriptures, theology, and the other pastoral studies in the course of the four ensuing years. This kind of courageous innovation toward the fulfillment of this decree on priestly formation is very much needed in our country.

The fathers' demand that all seminarians should study "under the tutelage of St. Thomas [Aquinas]" would seem to contradict the call to adapt the studies to the real needs of the local Church and to leave more specialized studies aside. One would like to see more emphasis on the indigenization of theology, using the philosophical traditions of the local peoples. Happily this is being done in some areas, notably in India with a Vedic philosophical base and in Japan with Taoist contributions. American seminaries do not yet seem to be sufficiently aware that the essentialist philosophical tradition is hardly relevant to the very existential thought of our people. This is in good part why even very sincere and devout Catholics are not hearing their pastors and why our separated brothers and sisters find theological dialogue with us so difficult.

DECREE CONCERNING THE ADAPTATION AND RENEWAL OF RELIGIOUS LIFE

I am not going to comment on this particular decree here. The matter is somewhat specialized, though a vital religious life is very important for the whole Church and the whole human family. Although the decree is quite short, it touches so vitally on my life experience that I could easily write a whole book on it — and probably will.

I am in Hong Kong as I write this. It is Easter Monday and the Cardinal invited all the men religious of the diocese to spend the day with him. After experiencing their oneness in the Risen Lord in the celebration of the Eucharist, each superior — there are sixteen different religious congregations of men in the diocese — gave a very brief expression of the corporate vision of his group in view of the extraordinary evolution taking place in the society within which this local Church lives. Then, after a festive meal, the Cardinal's men met the Provincials on the field of football. I won't tell you who won but in fact all were winners in what this kind of day does for the local Church.

DECREE CONCERNING THE APOSTOLATE OF THE LAITY

"By its very nature the Christian vocation is also a vocation to the apostolate." The Decree concerning the Apostolate of the Laity is undoubtedly the most important of the decrees implementing the Dogmatic Constitution concerning Church. It speaks to and concerns directly 99-plus percent of the People of God. If the Church is in the modern world, in the fabric of that world, it is because of the laity. This decree insists repeatedly on the laity's indispensable role in this regard. By its own particular definition of the laity, the decree excludes lay religious and speaks only of those who live fully in the secular world. I do not know how many of the laity actually had part in the writing and editing of the decree. It is one of the best for the clarity and conciseness of its presentation. As it proposes in the introduction, it considers the nature, character, variety, and basic principles of the lay apostolate and gives some pastoral directives. Nonetheless there are places where one feels the lay perspective is betrayed, a clerical hand is too exclusively at work.

The decree strongly affirms a creation theology with a good presentation of God's plan in the secular sphere. It struggles with finding the balance between the demands of a hierarchical Church that wields Christ's, God's authority and due human freedom. All humans, as humans are equal. None are secondary or derivative to any other class of fellow humans, though we have different roles. The laity are called to work *with* not *for* the clergy or hierarchy. One notes that in the many calls in the course of the decree for lay participation in the various activities of the Church there is never a call to participate in the government of the Church as such, even though it is affirmed that the layperson in virtue of baptism does participate in the kingly as well as the priestly and prophetic office of Christ.

The decree recognizes how much was already being done by laypeople and their organizations and affirms that, while seeking to open up many more possibilities. Having been in China I appreciate what it says about the vital role of the laity in a Church that has been deprived of the ordinary ministrations of priests and religious. More and more countries, I fear, and for reasons more selfish than the heavy hand of persecution, are going to be suffering this same deprivation or are already suffering from it. And the laity are stepping forward. The decree highlights lay collaboration ecumenically with other Christians and with other believers in bringing commonly held values to be effectively present in the social and political fabric of the modern world. The decree's insistent call to youth to bring their enthusiasms to the mission of Christ and his People is important, for therein lies the future. The decree lays due stress on the importance of a realistic spiritual grounding for effective apostolic action:

Since Christ in his mission from the Father is the fountain and source of the whole apostolate of the Church, the success of the lay apostolate depends upon the vital union that lay men and women have with Christ.... This life of intimate union with Christ in the Church is nourished by spiritual practices which are common to all the faithful, especially active participation in the sacred liturgy. These are to be used by the laity in such a way that while properly fulfilling their secular duties in the ordinary conditions of life, they do not disassociate union with Christ from that life....

Let the laypersons' religious program of life take its special quality from their status as married men and women and as family persons or as those who are unmarried or widowed, from their state of health, and from their professional and social activity. Let them not cease to develop earnestly the qualities and talents bestowed on them in accord with these conditions of life and make use of the gifts which they have received from Holy Spirit. (4)

For the layperson, apostolate begins in the home, and upon an active laity, spiritually, socially, and politically, the welfare of the home depends:

Christian husbands and wives are cooperators in grace and witnesses of faith on behalf of each other, their children, and all others in their household. They are the first to communicate the faith to their children and to educate them; by word and example they train their offspring for the Christian and apostolic life. They prudently help them in the choice of their vocation and carefully promote any religious calling which they may discern in them.

It has always been the duty of Christian couples but today it is the supreme task of their apostolate to manifest and prove by their own way of life the unbreakable and sacred character of the marriage bond, to affirm vigorously the right and duty of parents and guardians to educate children in a Christian manner, and to defend the dignity and lawful independence of the family. Let them and the rest of the faithful, therefore, cooperate with women and men of good will to ensure the preservation of these rights in civil legislation and to make sure that attention is paid to the needs of the family in government policies regarding housing, the education of children, working conditions, social security and taxes; and that in decisions affecting migrants the right to live together as a family is safeguarded. (11)

There is a lot of realism in this decree, as you can see. But at the same time, ideals are not lost sight of. This is again very evident in the decree's understanding of true "charity" or assistance to the poor:

While every exercise of the apostolate should take its origin and power from charity, some works by their very nature can become especially vivid expressions of this charity....

At the present time, when the means of communication have grown more rapid, the distances between peoples have been overcome in a sense, and the inhabitants of the whole world have become like members of a single family, these actions and works have grown much more urgent and extensive. These charitable enterprises can and should reach out to absolutely every person and every need. Wherever there are people in need of food and drink, clothing, housing, medicine, employment, education; wherever women and men lack the facilities necessary for living a truly human life or are tormented by hardships or poor health or suffer exile or imprisonment, there Christian charity needs to seek them out and find them, console them with eager care, and relieve them with the gift of help. This obligation is imposed above all upon every prosperous person and nation.

The exercise of this charity should be above any flaw and appear thus. There is to be seen in the neighbor the image of God, in which each is created, and Christ the Lord, to whom in truth is offered whatever is given to the indigent. The freedom and dignity of the person receiving help is to be respected with the greatest of humility. Let the purity of one's intention not be stained by any quest for personal advantage or by any thirst for domination. The demands of justice are first to be satisfied, lest the giving of what is due in justice be represented as the offering of a charitable gift. Not only the effects but also the causes of affliction need to be removed. Let help be given in such a way that the recipients may gradually be freed from dependence on others and become self-sufficient. (8)

This decree does not have much to say about "how to" —
which is proper for a decree addressed to all the Churches —
but it is full of challenge and possibility. Above all it shows
a full respect for the laity and for the temporal sphere within
which they as the People of God journey toward the Kingdom. And it recognizes the positive duty on the part of the
People of God to foster the temporal dimension of human
life:

God's plan for the world is that women and men work together to
restore the temporal sphere and to develop it unceasingly. Many
elements make up this temporal order: namely, the good things
of life and the prosperity of the family, culture, economic affairs,
the arts and professions, political institutions, international relations,
and other matters of this kind, as well as their development and
progress. All of these not only aid in the attainment of the ultimate
goal of women and men but also possess their own intrinsic value.
This value has been implanted in them by God whether they are
considered in themselves or as aspects of the whole temporal order.
"God saw all that he had made and it was very good" (Gen. 1:31).
This natural goodness of theirs takes on a special dignity as a result
of their relation to the human person, for whose service they were
created. Last of all, it has pleased God to unite all things, both natural and supernatural, in Christ Jesus "that in all things he may have
the first place" (Col. 1:18). This destination, however, not only does
not deprive the temporal order of its independence, its proper goals,
laws, resources, and significance for human welfare but rather per-
fects the temporal order in its own intrinsic vitality and excellence
and raises it to the level of the total vocation of women and men on
earth. (7)

3

From an Abundant Source

The Dogmatic Constitution concerning Divine Revelation is, along with the Dogmatic Constitution concerning Church, one of the fundamental or foundational pronouncements of the Second Vatican Council. It is a relatively short document, and at first glance it may not seem to be very significant. The ageing Scripture scholars who knew in their very bodies the blood, sweat, and tears that went into winning a hearing for the breakthroughs in their field that are solemnly endorsed in this constitution can most deeply savor the victory.

We take for granted now the more fulsome and human understanding of inspiration that is set forth here:

In composing the sacred books, God chose men and while employed by him they made use of their powers and abilities, so that with him acting in them and through them they, as true authors, consigned to writing everything and only those things which he wanted.

Therefore since everything asserted by the inspired authors or sacred writers must be held to be asserted by Holy Spirit, it follows that the books of Scripture must be acknowledged as teaching firmly, faithfully, and without error that truth which God wanted put

into the sacred writings for the sake of our salvation. Therefore "all
Scripture is inspired by God and useful for teaching, for reproving,
for correcting, for instruction in justice, that God's human person
may be perfect, equipped for every good work" (2 Tim. 3:16–17,
Greek text). (11)

And we realize that interpretation, the discernment "to see
clearly what God wanted to communicate to us," means to
"carefully investigate what meaning the sacred writers really
intended and what God wanted to manifest by means of their
words" (12). And we know that this means taking into account literary forms, the context of the writer's time and
culture, the content and unity of the whole of Scripture, the
living Tradition and what is called the analogy of faith, the
harmony that exists among the elements of faith.

Knowing the earlier work done by Protestant scholars that
first opened up the field of Scripture studies to these insights,
it might seem ungracious on the part of the Council not to
acknowledge this and express its appreciation and gratitude.
But the fathers held back from this because of the context
within which they were placing all their teaching on Scripture
in this constitution, a context that most Protestant scholars would find not only totally foreign but many would find
absolutely unacceptable. And herein lies the breakthrough
of this particular document, a breakthrough not so much
in doctrine as in the articulation of it, which nonetheless
indicated a new insight into what we had been holding.

The first schema that was presented at the first session
of the Council (and that was sent back for a rewrite by
a 60 percent vote) took a very different approach to the
matter. The title of the first chapter was "Two Sources of
Revelation," namely, Scripture and Tradition. This idea or
mode of expression, that there are two sources of Revelation,
was abandoned in the rewriting. Revelation is a manifesta-

tion by God of himself and of his will and designs. It has been granted to particular persons at particular times. (The constitution concerns itself only with public revelation, that destined by God for the good of all, not possible private revelations.) It has to be made know by the recipients. So long as this is passed on orally it is known as Tradition; written down under inspiration, it becomes Scripture. The two stand on equal footing. The constitution indicates this in its original Latin text by always capitalizing not only the word "Scripture," as we are generally accustomed to, but also always capitalizing the word "Tradition."

There is the one Revelation. "Through Tradition the Church's full canon of the sacred books is known and the sacred writings themselves are more profoundly understood and unceasingly made active in it" (8). And not all that is within the living Tradition has been recorded in the sacred books. "Consequently it is not from sacred Scripture alone that the Church draws its certainty about everything which has been revealed" (9).

Still more. Another element is added to the context: "Sacred Tradition and sacred Scripture form one sacred deposit of the word of God which is committed to the Church" (10). To the magisterium is committed the responsibility and duty of authentically interpreting both Scripture and Tradition:

The task of authentically interpreting the word of God, whether written or handed on, has been entrusted exclusively to the living, teaching office of the Church, whose authority is exercised in the name of Jesus Christ. This teaching office is not above the word of God but serves it, teaching only what has been handed on, listening to it devoutly, guarding it scrupulously, and explaining it faithfully by divine commission and with the help of Holy Spirit; it draws from this one deposit of faith everything which it presents for belief as divinely revealed.

It is clear, therefore, that sacred Tradition, sacred Scripture, and the teaching authority of the Church in accord with God's most wise design are so linked and joined together that one cannot stand without the others and that all together and each in its own way under the action of the one Holy Spirit contribute effectively to the salvation of souls. (10)

However, in the mind of the Council the bishops are not left alone in this important teaching role. The fathers themselves in the course of the elaboration of this constitution and all the other authoritative teachings of the Council were well aware of their dependence on the scholars and the many other advisors who served and assisted them. So they did not hesitate to declare:

... there is a growth in understanding of the realities and the words which have been handed down. This happens through the contemplation and study of believers who treasure these things in their hearts (cf. Lk. 2:19, 51), through the intimate understanding of the spiritual things they experience, and through the preaching of those who have received through episcopal succession the sure gift of truth. (8)

This significant passage, of course, has a much wider application. It indicates the way, in practice, that the development of doctrine takes place, a development that depends not only on the scholars and experts but on all the believers who reflect and pray and contemplate. Yet the bishops did not hesitate to affirm the "task of exegetes to work toward a better understanding and explanation of the meaning of sacred Scripture so that through preparatory study the judgment of the Church may mature."

Those who search out the intention of the sacred writers must, among other things, have regard for "literary forms." For truth is proposed and expressed in a variety of ways, depending on whether a

text is history of one kind or another, or whether its form is that
of prophecy, poetry, or some other type of speech. The interpreter
must investigate what meaning the sacred writer intended to express
and actually expressed in particular circumstances as he used contemporary literary forms in accordance with the situation in his own
time and culture. For the correct understanding of what the sacred
author wanted to assert, due attention must be paid to the custom-
ary and characteristic styles of perceiving, speaking, and narrating
which prevailed at the time of the sacred writer and to the customs
women and men normally followed at that period in their everyday
dealings with one another.

But, since holy Scripture must be read and interpreted according
to the same Spirit by whom it was written, no less serious attention
must be given to the content and unity of the whole of Scripture
if the meaning of the sacred texts is to be correctly brought to
light. The living tradition of the whole Church must be taken into
account along with the harmony which exists among the elements
of faith. (12)

It is easy to see how this teaching not only opens the door
wide to the development of doctrine but gives our understanding of the Revelation a breadth that is far from that of
those who hold for *sola Scriptura*, Scripture alone. There is
to be no new Revelation but there is so much more for us to
learn from the Revelation already given. We have seen specific instructions that were laid down in the divinely inspired
letters of St. Paul now set aside as being defined by a time and
a culture that is no longer ours. Women no longer must be
veiled and silent in Church. In the cultural advancement that
has come to recognize the full equality of women and men,
women can now with worthy dignity proclaim the Word of
the Lord. How much further will this development go? Will
Paul himself one day have a woman as his successor in the
college of the apostles? Who can say an a priori "no" and
still claim to be open to the Spirit and all the potential of the

development that this constitution proclaims. And who can say a certain "yes" while professing the same rightful docility to the guiding Spirit of the Church?

Another very significant passage in this short constitution which might be overlooked is found at the beginning of the fifth paragraph:

"The obedience of faith" (Rom. 16:26; cf. 1:5; 2 Cor. 10:5–6) must be given to God who reveals, an obedience by which women and men entrust their whole self freely to God, offering "the full submission of intellect and will to God who reveals"[1] and freely assenting to the truth revealed by him.

Pope John Paul II, one of the Council fathers, in his recent encyclical on Christian morality, "The Splendor of Truth" *Veritatis splendor,* has pointed to this as a correct and authentic understanding of the meaning of "fundamental option" for the Christian who has received the gift of faith.[2] The constitution goes on to point out that such an option, which is the ground of all our moral acts, can be made only with the help of God's grace and the effective guidance of the Spirit. When this is present, right action in the practical sphere of everyday decisions will necessarily follow, at least in regard to serious matters. We all fail in many little ways no matter what our fundamental option may be. But there will be no contradiction between our fundamental option and our particular actions in serious matters as an erroneous moral theology would pretend can exist.

The fuller appreciation of the role of Tradition and the development of doctrine found in this constitution in no way is meant to lessen Catholic appreciation for Scripture. If anything the Council did much to enhance our appreciation for

---

1. First Vatican Council, *Dogmatic Constitution concerning the Catholic Faith,* 3.

2. John Paul II, Encyclical Letter *Veritatis splendor,* August 6, 1993, no. 66.

the inspired word. The daily solemn enthronement of the sacred text at the sessions of the Council was most impressive and made clear how significant this sacred text was to the fathers and their deliberations. Today the Scriptures are enthroned in most Catholic churches, and it would be well if they were enthroned in every Catholic home as a Real Presence and a locus for the family to gather to hear the Lord and to be present to him in family prayer. In the final chapter the Council pushes the statement of its reverence for the sacred text about as far as it can:

The Church has always venerated the divine Scriptures just as it venerates the Body of the Lord, since from the table of both the Word of God and of the Body of Christ it unceasingly receives and offers to the faithful the bread of life, especially in the sacred liturgy. It has always regarded the Scripture together with sacred Tradition as the supreme rule of faith and will ever do so. For inspired by God and committed once and for all to writing, they impart the Word of God himself without change and make the voice of Holy Spirit resound in the words of the prophets and apostles. Therefore, like the Christian religion itself, all the preaching of the Church must be nourished and ruled by sacred Scripture. (21)

And then it goes on to exhort us to have a loving and intimate relationship with the holy Text: "For in the sacred books the Father who is in heaven meets his children with great love and speaks with them."

4

The Summit

The Constitution concerning the Sacred Liturgy was one of the first documents promulgated by the Second Vatican Council. That is why its first lines are very important. It is the first self-conscious statement of the conciliar fathers as to what they saw themselves to be about:

It is the goal of this sacred Council to intensify the daily growth of Catholics in Christian living, to make more responsive to the requirements of our times those Church observances which are open to adaptation, to nurture whatever can contribute to the unity of all who believe in Christ, and to strengthen those aspects of the Church which can help summon all of humankind into its embrace. (1)

The fathers also give expression to an initial sense of "the mystery of Christ and the real nature of the true Church," something they would, under Holy Spirit, explore much more deeply in the coming months and years of the Council.

It is of the essence of the Church that it be both human and divine, visible and yet invisibly endowed, eager to act and yet devoted to contemplation, present in this world and yet not at home in it. It is all these things in such a way that in it the human is directed and subordinated to the divine, the visible likewise to the invisible, action to contemplation, and this present world to that city yet to come, which we seek. (2)

The Council fathers were still quite self-conscious, as can be seen from the Latin title of the constitution: *Sacrosanctum Concilium,* the sacrosanct or most sacred Council. Latin style, or maybe rather Roman curial style, called for the adjective, which was retained throughout most of the Council in its documents. The fathers, at least many of them, as the Council progressed and they reflected more on the reality of the Church and themselves, began to see themselves more as the servants of the People of God and of the modern world, gathered and present like their Master, to serve and not to be served. But in this constitution, as in other places, we encounter instances where it seems the all-renewing Spirit ran into a prevailing, entrenched human spirit. For example, paragraph 48 opens: "The Church, therefore, earnestly desires that Christ's faithful...." Who are the authors identifying here as "the Church"? Obviously, themselves, the hierarchy, addressing themselves to the faithful, who are in fact 99-plus percent of the Church.

This self-centeredness of the assembled prelates is exposed in a summary glance through this important chapter on the Eucharist. The longest and most detailed number in the chapter is the one on what specifically concerns them: concelebration. Such detail is actually out of place in such a basic document as a conciliar constitution; it should have been left to the mandated instructions, where in fact it has been wholly repeated. And these details have quickly been left behind by the forward march of a living and vital Tradition. This self-centeredness is just another of the fruits of the almost total exclusion of the voice of the laity from the aula of the Council and even from its surrounding meetings.

The sheep are expected to hear the shepherds' voice but the shepherds seem to forget — at least in practice — that a good shepherd is always listening carefully to his sheep so that he can be immediately responsive to their needs.

Reflecting the earliest labors of the Council fathers, the constitution does not benefit from some of the deeper insight that the fathers gained as they worked on under Holy Spirit, although the Council had run half its course when this constitution was finally promulgated at the end of the second session. But this constitution was by far the best prepared of the pre-conciliar schemas. It benefited from a movement that had been going on for decades under the impetus of Holy Spirit.

In some ways the Council document sought to be a nozzle that directed the powerful current of the liturgical movement to the whole Church. At the same time it sought in some ways to restrain the movement and give it precise direction. However, the force of the movement has proved too strong to be restrained. Precisely where the constitution was most specific in its attempts to regulate the movement the very instructions it mandated set aside many of the restrictions of the constitution and let the current flow with a fuller energy.

Although the Constitution concerning the Sacred Liturgy came forth in fact before the other documents of the Council, it nonetheless is intimately connected with them and gives its own expression to their insights. The Dogmatic Constitution concerning Church sees the Church precisely as the People of God. And this constitution gives the liturgy, the prayer of the Church, to these People.

It did it, first of all, in granting the use of the vernacular languages in the celebration of the Mass and in all the other liturgical functions. Now the People of God can pray in their own sundry languages. The assembled People as well as priestly leadership can know exactly what is being said

or sung. Indeed, all can take part in determining and even creating this prayer of the People.

With a deep sense for the organic growth and ongoing weaving of Tradition, the Council fathers mandated that there should be some retention of the centuries-old Latin liturgy in language and forms, somewhat as the earlier move into vernacular — the third-century move from Greek to Latin — retained the Greek *Kyrie* within itself. Because, for the most part, this wisdom was not carried out in practice, there rose up a cry from among the People of God themselves for this. Unfortunately this cry for Tradition often became entwined with a plethora of mixed motives, oppositions arose, and positions hardened. A healing is yet needed in many places, so that we can fully recognize that we are all one in Christ, praying his prayer, and our diversities do not divide us.

Praying in China in recent years, where the local Church has been cut off from the Church universal since pre-Vatican times, I can appreciate what a difference the use of the vernacular has made in the prayer of the People of God. Yet not even the bamboo curtain has been able to withstand the powerful movement of the Spirit among the People. Held back for years because of the government's prohibition against importing books and at the same time its refusal to allow the Church presses to use paper to print the needed books, finally even the so-called Patriotic Church of China has officially moved into the vernacular at Easter 1993, using translations of the texts that have been produced in the post-conciliar period.

Returning the Cup to the People has also been a significant sign. The practice before the Council whereby only especially deputed sacristans (and these sometimes required to wear white gloves) could touch the Cup and then only when it was empty and previously "purified" by a cleric ir

major orders, while it sought in its strange way to inculcate reverence, was a terrible anti-sign of communion. Now every person consecrated by baptism can take the Cup of salvation and drink. The Council's restrictive legislation in regard to sharing the Cup has been quickly bypassed. Only practical considerations or a lack of appreciation of the fullness of the sign on the part of some ministers and communities make it still not a universal practice as it has always been in many of the Churches separated from Rome.

And so, who is this Church, these People of God who pray the liturgy? The Dogmatic Constitution concerning Church sees the People of God "subsisting" in the Roman Catholic Church but embracing all who have been baptized into Christ and in some way all who have said a "yes" to the Truth. The Decrees concerning Eastern Catholic Churches and concerning Ecumenism, with their later implementation in the Code of Canon Law, have tried to make some space for the liturgical realization of this enlarged understanding of the People of God. Here again law drags behind life. And life moves ahead. This is not wrong. For if the People of God with their liturgical leaders were fully expected to stay within the provisions of today's law, how could they ever step into tomorrow? How could there be a development of doctrine and practice? Recent liturgical law has generally left more room for creative leadership in the celebrations of the People of God. Nonetheless the powerful current of the Spirit within the liturgical movement ever rushes beyond this. "Where the Spirit is, there is freedom," says the Apostle Paul.

And it is in regard precisely to this Apostle's teaching that the liturgical renewal has had to implement the profound and profoundly important insights of the Dogmatic Constitution concerning Divine Revelation in regard to inspiration and interpretation of the Scriptures. As the early Church with its "Council of Jerusalem" had to decide what of the Mosaic

Law was still relevant, the Church of today with its ecumenical council and its implementation has had to look at Pauline
provisions and seek to determine, with the help of the now
fully recognized tools summarized in the Dogmatic Constitution concerning Divine Revelation, what is fully relevant.
In an age when the equality of the sexes is finally beginning to be universally acknowledged and women are playing
major roles in human society — think of recent prime ministers in India and England and presidents in Ireland and the
Philippines — women have set aside their veils and opened
their mouths in the assembly of the faithful. The development goes on. Is there anything that clearly prohibits women
from taking their place as equals beside deacons, priests, and
bishops? Certainly there were then as there are now voices
that would shout a strong "yes!": the example of the Lord
himself; twenty centuries of Tradition; ecumenical sensitivity
to the Orthodox Churches; the immense pastoral problems
that would arise in many parts of the Church; the sacramental symbolism; and maybe even the meaning of gender in the
light of the Persons of the Trinity. The Catholic Church is
a universal church; while there can be diverse practices in
different parts of the Church, it cannot move doctrinally on
a regional basis when there are theological questions to be
clarified. A guiding Spirit, in this case as in others, somehow
kept the question from arising within the Council in a demanding way that might have evoked a response consonant
with where the evolution was at that time but not sufficiently
open to where it might proceed. If the great inspired Apostle Paul had to challenge the first pope to his face on the
issue of food, we may yet have to see great prophetic voices
withstand popes of our time on the profoundly human and
evangelical issue of equality.

These issues are liturgical and it is in the liturgy where they
most immediately touch the life of the average layperson and

are most profoundly and constantly experienced. Yet they are far-reaching. They not only affect ecumenical rapprochement but they are where the Church meets the modern world and lives out the struggle of development of doctrine.

CONSTITUTION CONCERNING THE SACRED LITURGY

2. It is through the liturgy, especially the divine Eucharistic Sacrifice, that "the work of our redemption is exercised."[1] The liturgy is thus the outstanding means by which the faithful can express in their lives and manifest to others the mystery of Christ and the real nature of the true Church.... Day by day the liturgy builds up those within the Church into the Lord's holy temple, into a spiritual dwelling for God (cf. Eph. 2:21–22) – an enterprise which will continue until Christ's full stature is achieved (cf. Eph. 4:13). At the same time the liturgy marvelously fortifies the faithful in their capacity to preach Christ.

General Principles for the Restoration and Promotion of the Liturgy

5. God... "wishes all to be saved and come to the knowledge of the truth" (1 Tim. 2:4)...

7. To accomplish so great a work, Christ is always present in his Church, especially in its liturgical celebrations. He is present in the sacrifice of the Mass not only in the person of his minister, "the same one now offering, through the ministry of priests, who formerly offered himself on the cross,"[2] but especially under the Eucharistic species. By his power he is present in the sacraments, so that when a person baptizes it is really Christ himself who baptizes. He is present in his word, since it is he himself who speaks when the holy Scriptures are read in the Church. He is present, finally, when

---

1. *Roman Missal*, Ninth Sunday after Pentecost, Prayer over the offerings.
2. Council of Trent, Session 22.

the Church prays and sings, for he promised: "Where two or three are gathered together for my sake, there am I in the midst of them" (Mt. 18:20)....

Rightly, then, the liturgy is considered as an exercise of the priestly office of Jesus Christ. In the liturgy the sanctification of women and men is manifested by signs perceptible to the senses and is effected in a way which is proper to each of the signs. In the liturgy full public worship is performed by the Mystical Body of Jesus Christ, Head and members.

From this it follows that every liturgical celebration, because it is an action of Christ the priest and of his Body the Church, is a sacred action surpassing all others. No other action of the Church can match its claim to efficacy nor equal the degree of it....

9. The sacred liturgy does not exhaust the entire activity of the Church. Before women and men can come to the liturgy they must be called to faith and to conversion....

10. Nevertheless the liturgy is the summit toward which the activity of the Church is directed. At the same time it is the fountain from which all its power flows. For the goal of apostolic works is that all who are made sons and daughters of God by faith and baptism should come together to praise God in the midst of his Church, to take part in its sacrifice, and to eat the Lord's supper....

12. The spiritual life is not confined to participation in the liturgy. Christians are assuredly called to pray with their sisters and brothers but then must also enter into their chamber to pray to the Father in secret (cf. Mt. 6:6). Indeed, according to the teaching of the Apostle Paul, the Christian should pray without ceasing (cf. 1 Th. 5:17). We learn from the same Apostle that we must always carry about in our body the dying of Jesus so that the life of Jesus too may be made manifest in our bodily frame (cf. 2 Cor. 4:10–11). This is why we ask the Lord in the sacrifice of the Mass that "receiving the offering of the spiritual victim," he may fashion us to himself "as an eternal gift...."[3]

14. In the restoration and promotion of the sacred liturgy, full and active participation by all the people is the aim to be considered

---

3. Ibid., Monday after Pentecost, Secret Prayer.

before all else, for it is the primary and indispensable source from
which the faithful are to derive the true Christian spirit....

24. Sacred Scripture is of paramount importance in the celebration of the liturgy. For it is from Scripture that lessons are read and
explained in the homily and psalms are sung. The prayers, collects,
and liturgical songs are scriptural in their inspiration, and it is from
Scripture that actions and signs derive their meaning. Thus if the
restoration, progress, and adaptation of the sacred liturgy are to
be achieved, it is necessary to promote that warm and living love
for Scripture to which the venerable tradition of both Eastern and
Western rites gives testimony....

26. Liturgical services are not private functions, but are celebrations of the Church, which is the "sacrament of unity," a holy
people, united and organized under their bishops. Therefore liturgical services pertain to the whole body of the Church; they manifest
it and have effects upon it. They concern individual members of
the Church in different ways according to the diversity of holy
orders, functions, and degrees of participation.... In liturgical celebrations, whether as a minister or as one of the faithful, every person
should perform their role by doing solely and totally what the nature
of things and liturgical norms require of them.... Servers, lectors,
commentators, and members of the choir also exercise a genuine
liturgical function....

30. By way of promoting active participation, let the people
be encouraged to take part by means of acclamations, responses,
psalmody, antiphons, and songs, as well as by actions, gestures, and
bodily attitudes. And at the proper times let all observe a reverent
silence....

33. Although the sacred liturgy is above all the worship of the
divine majesty, it likewise contains abundant instruction for the faithful. For in the liturgy God speaks to his people and Christ is still
proclaiming his Gospel. And the people reply to God both by song
and prayer.

Moreover, the prayers addressed to God by the priest who presides over the assembly in the person of Christ are said in the name
of the entire holy people as well as of all present. And the visible

signs used by the liturgy to signify invisible divine things have been chosen by Christ or the Church. Thus, not only when things are read "which have been written for our instruction" (Rom. 15:4), but also when the Church prays or sings or acts, the faith of those taking part is nourished and their minds are raised to God so that they may offer him the worship which reason requires and more copiously receive his grace....

37. Even in the liturgy the Church has no wish to impose a rigid uniformity in matters which do not involve the faith or the good of the whole community. Rather it respects and fosters the spiritual adornments and gifts of the various races and peoples. Anything in their way of life that is not indissolubly bound up with superstition and error it studies with sympathy and, if possible, preserves intact. Sometimes in fact it admits such things into the liturgy, as long as they harmonize with its true and authentic spirit....

The Most Sacred Mystery of the Eucharist

It is as the praying People of God that Catholics most deeply meet the other Churches and ecclesial bodies and the modern world. Prayer is at the heart of this People; it is its very breath, especially this liturgical prayer. It is where this People is most truly one and one with its Head. Because of this oneness with him, it is the summit of the People's activity. Human activity has ultimate and divine relevance to the extent that it is an expression of true love. The crowning act of love that has brought all the People through to redemption and eternal life in its fullness is that offered on Calvary's hill by our Head. On the night before that climatic event he created for us a ritual act whereby we his People gathered around his priestly representative can truly make that act present, make it ours, and offer it as ours with him to the Father. Here is the summit. The whole of the liturgical renewal that this constitution seeks to enable the People to take possession of will be what it is meant to be if it leads the People of God to fully understand this sublime reality, integrate it into their lives, and live it to the full. For this, liturgical hours and a liturgical year are woven into our lives, liturgical music and liturgical art form and shape us and become a vehicle for us to express and deepen our Christian form. The value of each change and the mode of its implementation are to be carefully judged and evaluated in light of this central reality.

Though not labelled as such, as is the Pastoral Constitution concerning Church in the Modern World, this Constitution concerning the Sacred Liturgy is in fact a very pastoral constitution. Like the Code of Canon Law that has followed it, the chapters in the constitution begin with one or more doctrinal statements before getting to the practical provisions. These are very precious and most important. With magisterial authority they set forth very precisely the heart of the matter that is to govern all the following provisions and guide their implementation. Take for example paragraph 47, which opens the leading chapter on the Eucharist. Though only a few lines long it gives a rich theology of the Eucharist: It is a sacrament instituted by Christ at the Last Supper. Its purpose is to perpetuate his sacrifice, make it a continual reality for us in our midst, through time, right until the end, until he comes. It is a memorial, a power to make present, given to the Church, which makes not only his death but also his resurrection present, as a sacrament of devotion, his devotion to us and a way in which we can express our devotion to him. It is also a sign of unity, of all of us together and of him with us; it is a *vinculum,* a chain of love that actually ties us together. It is a paschal meal, the continuation and fulfillment of that celebrated through the centuries before he came, in which he is actually eaten and we are filled with grace and given a concrete pledge of our future glory.

All of this is stated in fewer lines than it took me to state it here. All very seminal, capable of much expansion. Reflection on this short paragraph can be a powerful and effective preparation for one who wants to celebrate the Eucharist well and fully. The next paragraph offers moral principles or principles for making these theological principles come alive in our lives, communally and individually, reaching toward the consummation when God will be "all in all." Only after setting these forth does the chapter go on to specifics about the renewal of the Eucharist.

The selected paragraphs of the Constitution concerning the Sacred Liturgy offered here are by preference those that set forth the theological principles, though the others are not wholly neglected, for this would not do justice to what is, as we have said, truly a pastoral constitution.

47. At the Last Supper, on the night when he was betrayed, our Savior instituted the Eucharistic Sacrifice of his Body and Blood. He did this in order to perpetuate the sacrifice of the Cross throughout the centuries until he should come again, and so to entrust to his beloved spouse, the Church, a memorial of his death and resurrection: a sacrament of devotion, a sign of unity, a bond of charity, a paschal banquet in which Christ is eaten, the inner person is filled with grace, and a pledge of future glory is given to us.

48. The Church, therefore, earnestly desires that Christ's faithful will not be present at this mystery of faith as strangers or silent spectators. On the contrary, through a proper appreciation of the rites and prayers let them participate knowingly, devoutly, and actively. Let them be instructed by God's Word and be refreshed at the table of the Lord's Body. Let them give thanks to God. By offering the immaculate Victim, not only through the hands of the priest but also with him, let them learn to offer themselves. Through Christ the Mediator, let them be drawn day by day into an ever closer union with God and with each other, so that finally God may be all in all....

The Sacraments and Sacramentals

59. The purpose of the sacraments is to sanctify women and men, to build up the body of Christ, and to give worship to God. Because they are signs they also instruct. They not only presuppose faith but by words and objects they also nourish, strengthen, and express it. That is why they are called "sacraments of faith." They do indeed impart grace but in addition the very act of celebrating them disposes the faithful most effectively to receive this grace in a fruitful manner to worship God duly and to practice charity....[4]

60. In addition the Church has instituted sacramentals. These are sacred signs which bear a resemblance to the sacraments: they signify effects, particularly of a spiritual kind, which are obtained through the Church's intercession. By them women and men are disposed to receive the chief effect of the sacraments and various occasions in life are rendered holy.

61. Thus for well-disposed members of the faithful the liturgy of the sacraments and sacramentals sanctifies almost every event in their lives. They are given access to the stream of divine grace which flows from the paschal mystery of the passion, death, and resurrection of Christ, the fountain from which all sacraments and sacramentals draw their power. There is hardly any proper use of material things which cannot thus be directed toward the sanctification of women and men and the praise of God....

The Divine Office

83. Christ Jesus, high priest of the new and eternal covenant, taking human nature, introduced into this earthly exile that hymn which is sung throughout all ages in the halls of heaven. He joins the entire community of humankind to himself, associating it with his own singing of this canticle of divine praise. For he continues his priestly work through the agency of his Church, which is ceaselessly engaged in praising the Lord and interceding for the salvation of the

---

4. There is a concise doctrinal presentation of each of the sacraments in the Dogmatic Constitution concerning Church, n. 11.

whole world. This it does not only by celebrating the Eucharist but also in other ways, especially by praying the divine office.

84. By tradition going back to the early Christian times, the divine office is arranged so that the whole course of the day and night is made holy by praises of God. Therefore when this wonderful song of praise is worthily rendered by priests and others who are deputed for this purpose by Church ordinance or by the faithful praying together with the priest in an approved form, then it is truly the voice of the bride addressing her bridegroom; it is the very prayer which Christ himself, together with his Body, addresses to his Father.

85. Hence all who perform this service are not only fulfilling a duty of the Church but also are sharing in the greatest honor accorded to Christ's spouse, for by offering these praises to God they are standing before God's throne in the name of the Church....

88. Because the purpose of the office is to sanctify the day, the traditional sequence of the hours is to be restored so that as far as possible they may once again be genuinely related to the time of the day at which they are prayed. Moreover, it will be necessary to take into account the modern conditions in which daily life has to be lived, especially by those who are called to labor in apostolic works....

The Liturgical Year

102. The Church is conscious that it must celebrate the saving work of its divine Spouse by devoutly recalling it on certain days throughout the course of the year. Every week on the day it has called the Lord's day, it keeps the memory of his resurrection. In the supreme solemnity of Easter it also makes an annual commemoration of the resurrection along with the Lord's blessed passion.

Within the cycle of the year, moreover, it opens out the whole mystery of Christ, not only from his incarnation and birth until his ascension but also as it is reflected in the day of Pentecost and in the expectation of a blessed, hoped-for return of the Lord.

Recalling thus the mysteries of redemption, the Church opens to the faithful the riches of its Lord's powers and merits so that these are in some way made present at all times and the faithful are enabled to lay hold of them and be filled with saving grace.

103. In celebrating this annual cycle of Christ's mysteries the Church honors with special love the Blessed Mary, Mother of God, who is joined by an inseparable bond to the saving work of her Son. In her the Church holds up and admires the most excellent fruit of the redemption and joyfully contemplates, as in a faultless model, that which it itself wholly desires and hopes to be.

104. The Church has also included in the annual cycle days devoted to the memory of the martyrs and the other saints. Brought to perfection by the manifold grace of God and already in possession of eternal salvation, they sing God's perfect praise in heaven and offer prayers for us. By celebrating the passage of these saints from earth to heaven the Church proclaims the paschal mystery as achieved in the saints who have suffered and been glorified with Christ. It proposes them to the faithful as examples who draw all to the Father through Christ, and through their merits it pleads for God's favors.

105. Finally in the various seasons of the year and according to its traditional discipline, the Church completes the formation of the faithful by means of pious practices for soul and body, by instruction, prayer, and works of penance and of mercy....

106. By an apostolic tradition which took its origin from the very day of Christ's resurrection, the Church celebrates the paschal mystery every eighth day. With good reason this then bears the name of the Lord's day or the day of the Lord. For on this day Christ's faithful should come together into one place so that, by hearing the word of God and taking part in the Eucharist, they may call to mind the passion, the resurrection, and the glorification of the Lord Jesus and may thank God who "has begotten us again, through the resurrection of Jesus Christ from the dead unto a living hope" (1 Pet. 1:3). Hence the Lord's day is the original feast day and it should be promoted and made a part of the devotion of the faithful in such a

way that it may become in fact a day of joy and of freedom from
work....

110. During Lent, penance should not be only internal and individual but also external and social. The practice of penance should
be fostered according to the possibilities of the present day and of
a given area as well as those of the individual's circumstances.... In
any event let the paschal fast be kept sacred. It should be observed
everywhere on Good Friday and where possible prolonged through
Holy Saturday, so that with an uplifted and open spirit the faithful
might enter into the joys of the Sunday of the resurrection....

Sacred Music

112. The musical tradition of the universal Church is a treasure of
immeasurable value, greater even than that of any other art.... Holy
Scripture indeed has bestowed praise upon sacred song (cf. Eph.
5:19; Col. 3:16) and the same may be said of the Fathers of the
Church....

Sacred music pertains more to the realm of the holy to the degree that it is intimately linked with liturgical action, expresses prayer
more beautifully, promotes unanimity, and enriches sacred rites with
heightened solemnity. The Church indeed approves of all forms
of true art and admits them into divine worship when they show
appropriate qualities....

119. Since in certain parts of the world, especially in mission
lands, there are peoples who have their own musical tradition which
plays a great part in their religious and social life, this music is to
be properly appreciated and given a suitable place both in forming
their religious sense and in their worship which must be adapted to
their native genius....

Sacred Art and Sacred Furnishings

123. The Church has not adopted any particular style of art as
its own. It has admitted fashions from every period according to
the natural talents and circumstances of people and the needs of

the various rites. Thus in the course of the centuries it has brought into being a treasury of art which must be very carefully preserved. The art of our own days, coming from every race and region, shall also be given free scope in the Church, provided that it adorns the sacred buildings and sacred rites with due honor and reverence. It will thereby be able to contribute its own voice to that wonderful chorus of praise sung in honor of the catholic faith by great women and men in times gone by....

The Constitution concerning the Sacred Liturgy does have its weaknesses. One of them is its overattention to the liturgy proper to the Western or Roman Church, again giving some justification to the complaint of Eastern hierarchs that this gathering was more a synod of the West than a truly ecumenical council. Those provisions which pertain to the particular liturgical practice of the West should have been left to later instructions — where indeed they are all again treated — as should have been much of the detail that sometimes comes into the constitution's provisions. Such detail does not belong in a constitution and, of course, has quickly become dated. These betray the overcautious attitude of the fathers, the common lack of immediate pastoral experience in and among the people, and the desire of the Roman curia to keep things under control. It is, indeed, a bit surprising that a council that brought forth so fully the office of bishops should yet have approved a document that constantly subjected them and their national conferences to the supervision of a Roman congregation.

But we need to keep in mind that this document was completed while the Dogmatic Constitution concerning Church was still in process. Again, the insistence on rubrics and the requirement that the Roman rubrics be reproduced in all local liturgical books are an endorsement of that controlling attitude. The constitution did call for the simplification of the rites, but unfortunately did not call for a simplification of the rubrics. The new Roman Ritual, a thick volume, contains far more rubrics than liturgical text. This overlegislation does not serve. The exasperated priest will simply put the volume aside and go ahead on his own. If he has an inner feel for the liturgy, this might be good. If he does not, it can produce a terrible mess. And detailed rubrics would not really help in this case. The constitution repeatedly insists on the importance of the rites clearly expressing what they have to say. A strong, clear statement of informing principles and a few basic rubrics will serve us far better.

The appendix of this constitution is a wonderful statement of the Church's presence to the modern world and its fellow Christians in dialogue. The Church is ready to accept a new calendar if secular society wants it, provided the Catholic's brothers and sisters in the other Churches are comfortable with it. It stands strong for the uninterrupted seven-day week but even here it is ready to yield if the reasons are weighty enough. If the wonderful attitude that is found here prevails in all the Church's encounters with the "separated brothers and sisters" and the human community at large, the possibilities and promises of the Council will indeed be realized.

Revision of the Calendar

The Second Ecumenical Council of the Vatican recognizes the importance of the wishes expressed by many concerning the assignment of the feast of Easter to a fixed Sunday and concerning an unchanging calendar. Having carefully considered the effects which could result from the introduction of a new calendar the Council declares:

1. It would not object if the feast of Easter were assigned to a particular Sunday of the Gregorian Calendar provided that those whom

it may concern give their consent, especially the brothers and sisters who are not in communion with the Apostolic See.

2. The Council likewise declares that it does not oppose efforts designed to introduce a perpetual calendar into civil society. But among the various systems which are being devised for establishing a perpetual calendar and introducing it into civil society the Church has no objection only in the case of those systems which would retain and safeguard a seven-day week including Sunday, without the introduction of any days outside the week. In other words the sequence of seven-day weeks should remain unbroken. Only the weightiest of reasons, acknowledged as such by the Apostolic See, would make the contrary acceptable.

On the whole the Constitution concerning the Sacred Liturgy is an open document, looking to the future, encouraging the growth of authenticity and catholicity among the People of God. To date it has been one of the most effective of the Council documents. It has challenged and continues to challenge the People of God very concretely in their everyday life in the local community. Priests and the lay leadership in the parishes need an ever-renewed courage and energy to live this challenge to the full and thus renew the life of the People of God most intimately in a way that will give impetus to living all the other calls to renewal found in the other documents of the Council. Our celebration of the liturgy brings us to the summit of Christian life while remaining a vitalizing source for all the rest of our life in Christ.

5

On to Today...
and Tomorrow's Today

The Pastoral Constitution concerning Church in the Modern World is the document that most properly belongs to the Second Vatican Council. We might say it came spontaneously out of the heart of the Council fathers. It was not planned. It was in no way on the agenda of the preparatory commissions. In a way it consummates and completes the work of the fathers. But most important: it is the Council's charter into the future. It is a very explicit call for the work of the Council to go on.

The title tells us much. It is a "constitution," that is, it tells us what constitutes the Church, what makes it to be. But more precisely it is a "pastoral constitution": it tells us what makes the Church a pastor, a good shepherd — how the Church is and functions pastorally.

It locates the Church: "the Church *in* the modern world." The Church no longer sees itself apart from the world, outside the world, and certainly not as standing in opposition to the world. The Church is in the world. And not just in the world as something standing within it, like a church building might stand in the middle of a city or town. The Church is woven into the very fabric of the world. Those who make up the Church are those who make up the modern world. They are not coterminous, Church and world. Many of those in the modern world are not yet fully incorporated into the Church. And the Church has members beyond this world: that great assembly of graduates, the blessed in heaven and the suffering in purgatory, and above all its glorious Head, whose plenitude embraces all the fullness of the world and more.

Yet the Church identifies very deeply with the world, and precisely the modern world. The Church now sees it not as something to be decried and shunned, but rather as a worthy dialogue partner — a partner not only worth talking with but even worth working with where our goals coalesce.

This is the real key to this very important document of the Council fathers: dialogue. A dialogical openness to all. Far more important is it to get hold of this fundamental attitude and make it our own than to acquire an intellectual grasp of all the doctrine to be found within this very rich constitution. After affirming its solidarity with humankind and humankind's ongoing history, the Council speaks to all: "not only the sons and daughters of the Church and to all who invoke the name of Christ, but to the whole of humanity." It affirms then its desire to enter into a conversation. Realizing that the world does not possess all that the Church does, it is willing to meet the world on the world's own ground: "the pivotal point of our total presentation will be the human person, whole and entire, body and soul, heart and conscience, mind and will." While the Church is of its very nature theocentric and Christocentric, in this conversation it is willing to be anthropocentric.

Yet, as an open and honest dialogical partner, it does not keep any hidden agendas. The Council frankly states what it sees it has to bring to the conversation over and above its human experience: "light kindled from the Gospel" as well as all those other saving resources the Church has received from its Founder under the guidance of Holy Spirit. Moreover it makes clear what is in fact its ultimate goal in reaching out and seeking to enter into this conversation: "to carry forward the work of Christ himself under the lead of the befriending Spirit. Christ entered this world to give witness to the truth, to save and not to sit in judgment, to serve and not to be served."

As the fathers will affirm, though, again and again in the course of this very lengthy initiation of the conversation, this goal is in no way contrary to the innate goals of the human individual or society but rather is the enhancing fulfillment of them. This is what the world needs to hear — and perhaps we also. For I am afraid even some professing Christians have perceived the demands of their faith as being in some way inimical to a full human development. And indeed, the faith may have been presented to us in some truncated way that would have also truncated our humanity. It is a tremendously powerful humanism that is presented in this document, the humanism of the divine Creator, who made the human person and made that person not only for complete fulfillment but for divinization, for a participation in the Creator's own divinity. That is where the Church as a dialogue partner can open up vistas for the modern person that are beyond his or her wildest dreams.

The fathers take a few pages to put their document in context. The Introductory Statement is one of very deep compassion, in the literal sense of that word: a feeling with. It takes us back to the Latin title of this document. According to the age-old custom, Church documents are usually

called by the first few words of the Latin text. Therefore these
words are usually very carefully chosen to express something
of the basic tenor of the document. This constitution is called
Gaudium et spes: Joy and hope. This is indeed what the fathers see the Church is meant to bring to the modern world:
joy, as it enters into the dialogue and shows moderns that
all that they hope for is meant to be fulfilled, and more; and
hope, Christ through his Church offers a way to that fulfillment. But before unfolding the source of that hope, the
fathers indicate that they are more than aware of the anguish
that besets the modern world. Profound and rapid changes
are causing a transformation in our social and cultural fabric
that threatens to get totally out of control and cause such im-
balances that they will lead to disaster if they are not soon
much more effectively addressed. A communication explo-
sion is giving us more than we can handle, getting ahead of
our thought and value systems, depriving us of time for the
spirit.

It is painful to read here the long descriptions of the modern world with its problems and challenges, its hopes and
it fears and its basic questions, and, realizing that this was
written almost thirty years ago, to know that things have not
changed. If anything they have just continued to rush down
the same routes toward the same disasters, some of which are
already being realized in various degrees: the deadly famines,
the tragic and chaotic ethnic wars, the impoverishing arms
race that has led America from being the largest creditor nation in the world to becoming in a very short space of time
the largest debtor nation. And yet we continue to spend an
enormous part of our budget on developing still more prob-
lematic weaponry while more and more of our people sleep
in the streets and eat out of garbage cans.

PASTORAL CONSTITUTION CONCERNING CHURCH IN THE MODERN WORLD

1. The joy and the hope, the grief and the anxiety of men and women of this age, especially those who are poor or in any way afflicted, these too are the joy and hope, the grief and anxiety of the followers of Christ. Indeed, nothing genuinely human fails to raise an echo in their hearts. For theirs is a community composed of men and women. United in Christ, they are led by Holy Spirit in their journey to the Kingdom of their Father and they have welcomed the news of salvation which is meant for every person. That is why this community realizes that it is truly and intimately linked with humankind and its history.

2. Hence this Second Vatican Council, having probed more profoundly into the mystery of the Church, now addresses itself without hesitation, not only to the sons and daughters of the Church and to all who invoke the name of Christ, but to the whole of humanity....

3. Though humankind today is struck with wonder at its own discoveries and its power, it often raises anxious questions about the current trend of the world, about the place and role of the human person in the universe, about the meaning of the human's individual and collective striving, and about the ultimate destiny of reality and of humanity. Hence, giving witness and voice to the faith of the whole People of God gathered together by Christ, this Council can provide no more eloquent proof of its solidarity with the entire human family with which it is bound up, as well as its respect and love for that family, than by engaging with it in conversation about these various problems.

The Council brings to humankind light kindled from the Gospel and puts at its disposal those saving resources which the Church herself, under the guidance of Holy Spirit, received from its Founder. For the human person deserves to be preserved; human society deserves to be renewed. Hence the pivotal point of our total presentation will be the human person, whole and entire, body and soul, heart and conscience, mind and will.

This sacred Synod proclaims the exalted destiny of the human person and champions the godlike seed which has been sown within that person. It offers to humankind the honest assistance of the Church in fostering that brotherhood and sisterhood of all humans which corresponds to this destiny of theirs. Inspired by no earthly ambition, the Church seeks but a solitary goal: to carry forward the work of Christ himself under the lead of the befriending Spirit. Christ entered this world to give witness to the truth, to save and not to sit in judgment, to serve and not to be served.

The Situation of Humans in the Modern World

In an extraordinarily good example of an open dialogical attitude, the Council takes great pains to let the modern world know how it sees that world, so that its dialogue partner can have every opportunity to correct any misconceptions it may be harboring about our positions.

4. Today the human race is passing through a new stage of its history. Profound and rapid changes are spreading by degrees around the whole world. Triggered by the intelligence and creative energies of men and women, these changes recoil upon them, upon their decisions and desires, both individual and collective, and upon their manner of thinking and acting with respect to things and to people. Hence we can already speak of a true social and cultural transformation, one which has repercussions on religious life as well.

Never has the human race enjoyed such an abundance of wealth, resources, and economic power. Yet a huge proportion of the world's citizens is still tormented by hunger and poverty, while countless members suffer from total illiteracy. Never before today have women and men been so keenly aware of freedom, yet at the same time, new forms of social and psychological slavery make their appearance. Although the world of today has a very vivid sense of its unity and of how one person depends on another in needful solidarity, it is most grievously torn into opposing camps by conflicting forces. For political, social, economic, racial, and ideological disputes still continue bitterly and with them the peril of a war which would reduce everything to ashes....

10. In the face of the modern development of the world, an ever-increasing number of people are raising the most basic questions or recognizing them with a new sharpness: What is a human? What is this sense of sorrow, of evil, of death, which continues to exist despite so much progress? What is the purpose of these victories, purchased at so high a cost? What can the human person offer to society, what can a person expect from it? What follows this earthly life?

The Church believes that Christ, who died and was raised up for all, can through his Spirit offer women and men the light and the strength to measure up to their supreme destiny....

The constitution is divided into two parts. The first "lays the foundation for the relationship between the Church and the world and provides the basis for dialogue between them." The second then inaugurates the dialogue, looking at some of the "particularly urgent needs characterizing the present age, needs which go to the roots of the human race." Three of the four chapters of the first part seek to lay out in detail how the Church sees the modern world, or rather the "pivotal point" of that world: the human person. The first chapter speaks of the dignity of the human person; the second, of the person's social or communal nature: the community of humankind; the third, of the human person's activity. At the beginning of the fourth chapter the fathers note that they have already amply laid out how they see the Church in itself in the Dogmatic Constitution concerning Church, and so they dedicate this chapter to simply situating the Church in the modern world.

In passing let us note that there is some ambiguity lurking around this document. As we have seen, the Dogmatic Constitution concerning Church has made it clear that the concept of Church expands beyond the confines of the Roman Catholic Church. The fathers gathered in Council are rightly the spokesmen for the Roman Catholic Church, but are they for Church as such? Or are we to understand them to mean "Roman Catholic Church" when they say "Church" in this document. I suspect not, for they do at times explicitly speak of Roman Catholics, and, on the other hand, they do speak at times for all Christians. In any case, we need to recall again that we are Church; and insofar as we are Christians and we are Church and we are Catholics, we need to listen critically and ask: Do the fathers of the Council speak accurately for us? And this in two senses: Are they saying what we actually know or believe, or are they saying what we should know or believe, what we need to grow into? We may conclude that neither is true — for this is not all infallible teaching and, as the fathers themselves note, "It happens rather frequently, and legitimately so, that with equal sincerity some of the faithful will disagree with others on a given matter." But we at least owe this solemn magisterium serious attention and must be slow to part from it.

But let us return to our document. The intent of the fathers in the first part of the constitution is to lay down a solid foundation for an ongoing conversation. However, they actually do enter into the conversation without delay. In each chapter they bring from the revelation an insight into the matter at hand that offers the modern world an opportunity to expand its vista and discover an even more sublime fulfillment of its aspirations.

The modern world in its better moments wants to exalt the human person and preserve human dignity above all. The Church tells the world that indeed this is the divine plan and much more, for the Lord has actually made the human to God's own image and would raise this creature to a sharing of the divine nature.

The modern world sees technology making the human family more and more closely one and interdependent. The Church tells of a oneness in the redemption of Christ whereby humans are called to be one with one another in a oneness like unto that absolute oneness of Father, Son, and Holy Spirit. The Church also brings to this discussion centuries of experience in creating and living worldwide community, an experience that is invaluable. For such community, though, all must be accepted as equals. It is here we find one of the areas where the thinking of the modern world has evolved in the intervening thirty years and challenges the Church anew. The world has become much more sensitive to the deep-seated prejudice and blatant discrimination that has infested it in regard to women. It is also growing in awareness of the hateful discrimination present regarding sexual orientation. With respect to these issues today's ecclesial leadership wants to adopt the dialogical openness espoused by the Council.

As to human activity, not only does the Church's shared Revelation foster all that can better the world and the lot of the human family but, telling of a Creator, it elevates human activity to being a participation in the creative activity of God, bringing that activity toward its completion. There is no opposition between Revelation and a true humanism; in fact, Revelation calls us to a sublime humanism. This is something of the Good News the Church wants to bring to the conversation with the modern world.

In this first part, each chapter ends with a section on Christ. He is indeed the answer: Christ as the New Man; as the Incarnate Word, the key to full human solidarity; as the Lord of a new heaven and a new earth; and as the Alpha and Omega. These four sections offer us a tremendously rich Christology, the Christology of Vatican II. Theologians can work with them to bring us forward in our understanding of our Lord Christ. In the meantime we can well use them for very fruitful *lectio,* deep, loving, meditative reading, or rather listening to what the Spirit is saying to the Churches today about Christ, the Lord of the modern world.

Toward the end of the fourth chapter, which has been talking about the role of the Church in the modern world, the fathers note that the Church has "to set forth the Gospel in a way that it can be grasped by all as well as satisfy the needs of the learned." Indeed they go on to say "this accommodated preaching of the revealed Word ought to remain the law of all evangelization" (44). Much of what the Council has had to say about adaptation, inculturation, or interculturation, has been applied primarily to Asia and Africa, to the emerging Church in the emerging nations. Undoubtedly it is here that the need is most evident. Jesus imparted his Revelation in a very simple Semitic language. It took several centuries and many fierce controversies to find the adequate way to express this Revelation in Greco-Roman philosophical concepts. Then with few exceptions — one thinks of Kerala in India where St. Thomas early brought the faith — this became normative. One had to virtually become a Greco-Roman in one's thinking patterns to become a Christian. There is no surprise then that preaching the Gospel has made such little progress outside of the European sphere.

With the Second Vatican Council the Church makes a bid to become truly "catholic." And progress is being made in India with the use of ancient Vedic philosophy and in Japan with Taoist thinking. One of the leading spiritual masters in Japan, who was a convert from Buddhism, told me that after years of scholastic study he came to truly know Christ and Christian belief only when he learned Hebrew and was able to read the Scriptures in this language or read the Greek Scriptures in the light of the Hebrew. Then he contacted the Revelation directly as a Japanese and not indirectly through Western concepts and constructs.

What I would like to point out here is this: We in the West, especially in the United States, have seen this call to adaption as directed primarily to our brothers and sisters in Africa and Asia. We have seen it as having little application to ourselves. Our magisterial teaching continues to couch itself in the essentialist concepts of medieval scholastic philosophy. And the result is a lack of communication. This is why many truly dedicated Catholics are not hearing the magisterium. Perhaps no Catholic has had such impact on the American faithful as has the Cistercian monk Fr. Louis, Thomas Merton. Merton was very traditional in his religious thought. He had studied his scholastic philosophy and theology well in preparation for his ordination to the ministerial priesthood. Yet he was at heart an existentialist, and he wrote as an existentialist. And that is why he could be so well heard by American Catholics and many Europeans as well. Americans are existentialists in their outlook and thought patterns. And the American Church has to take on the responsibility to proclaim the Gospel in existential terms if it hopes to communicate with and be heard by the modern American. The personalist philosophy of Pope John Paul II might also be readily heard if it were well translated. "Accommodated preaching of the revealed Word ought to remain the law of all evangelization."

Let us look at these first four chapters of the constitution, or at least some portions of them:

The Dignity of the Human Person

12. According to the almost unanimous opinion of believers and unbelievers alike, all things on earth should be related to the human person as their center and crown.... Sacred Scripture teaches that women and men were created "to the image of God," are capable of knowing and loving their Creator, and were appointed by him as master of all earthly creatures that they might subdue them and use them to God's glory.... By their innermost nature women and men

are social beings, and unless they relate themselves to others they can neither live nor develop their potential....

13. Sin has diminished women and men, blocking their path to fulfillment. The call to grandeur and the depths of misery are both a part of human experience....

14. Though made of body and soul, the human person is one. ...Women and men are not wrong when they regard themselves as superior to bodily concerns and as more than a speck of nature or a nameless constituent of the human city. For by their interior qualities they outstrip the whole sum of mere things....

15. The intellectual nature of the human person is perfected by wisdom and needs to be....Through the gift of Holy Spirit women and men come by faith to the contemplation and appreciation of the divine plan.

16. Conscience is the most secret core and sanctuary of a human person. There each is alone with God, whose voice echoes in one's depths. In a wonderful manner conscience reveals that law which is fulfilled by love of God and neighbor. In fidelity to conscience, Christians are joined with the rest of the human family in the search for truth and for the genuine solution to the numerous problems which arise in the life of individuals and from social relationships....Conscience frequently errs from invincible ignorance without losing its dignity. The same cannot be said of a person who cares but little for truth and goodness or of a conscience which by degrees grows practically sightless as a result of habitual sin....

17. Only in freedom can women and men direct themselves toward goodness. Our contemporaries make much of this freedom and pursue it eagerly and rightly so....

18. It is in the face of death that the riddle of human existence becomes most acute....Although the mystery of death utterly beggars the imagination, the Church has been taught by divine revelation and it itself firmly teaches that women and men have been created by God for a blissful purpose beyond the reach of earthly misery....

Christ as the New Man

22. The truth is that only in the mystery of the incarnate Word is the mystery of the human truly made clear. For Adam, the first man, was a figure of him who was to come, Christ the Lord. Christ, the final Adam, by the revelation of the mystery of the Father and his love, fully reveals us to ourselves and makes our supreme calling clear.... To the sons and daughters of Adam he restores the divine likeness which had been disfigured from the first sin onward. Since in him human nature was assumed, not preempted, by that very fact it was given a sublime dignity in us too. For by his incarnation the Son of God has united himself in some fashion with every man and woman. He worked with human hands, he thought with a human mind, acted by human choice and loved with a human heart. Born of the Virgin Mary, he has truly been made one of us, like us in all things except sin.

As an innocent lamb he merited life for us by the free shedding of his own blood. In him God reconciled us to himself and among ourselves. He delivered us from bondage to the devil and sin, so that each of us can say with the Apostle: The Son of God "loved me and gave himself up for me" (Gal. 2:20). By suffering for us he not only provided us with an example for our imitation. He blazed a trail, and if we follow it, life and death are made holy and take on a new meaning.... All this holds true not only for Christians, but for all persons of good will in whose hearts grace works in an unseen way. For since Christ died for all and since the ultimate vocation of women and men is in fact one and divine, we ought to believe that Holy Spirit, in a manner known only to God, offers to every person the possibility of being associated with this paschal mystery.

Such is the mystery of the human person, and it is a great one, as seen by believers in the light of Christian revelation. Through Christ and in Christ, light is thrown on the enigma of sorrow and death. Apart from his Gospel they overwhelm us. Christ has risen, destroying death by his death. He has lavished life upon us so that as sons and daughters in the Son we can cry out in the Spirit: Abba, Father!

The Human Community

23. One of the salient features of the modern world is the growing interdependence of human beings, a development very largely promoted by modern technical advances. Nevertheless, brotherly and sisterly dialogue among women and men does not reach its perfection on the level of technical progress but on the deeper level of interpersonal relationships. These demand a mutual respect for the full spiritual dignity of the person. Christian revelation contributes greatly in the promotion of this communion between persons and at the same time leads us to a deeper understanding of the laws of social life which the Creator has written into the human's spiritual and moral nature....

25. The beginning, the subject, and the goal of all social institutions is and ought to be the human person, which for its part and by its very nature stands completely in need of social life....Through their dealings with others, through reciprocal duties, and through brotherly and sisterly dialogue, women and men develop all their gifts and are able to rise to their destiny.

Among those social ties which women and men need for their development some, like the family and political community, relate with greater immediacy to their inmost nature. Others originate rather from their free decision. In our era, for various reasons, reciprocal ties and mutual dependencies increase day by day and give rise to a variety of associations and organizations both public and private. This development, which is called socialization, while certainly not without its dangers, brings with it many advantages with respect to consolidating and increasing the qualities of human persons and safeguarding their rights....

26. The common good — the sum of those conditions of social life which allow social groups and their individual members fuller and more ready access to their own fulfillment — today takes on an increasingly universal complexion and consequently involves rights and duties with respect to the whole human race. Every social group must take account of the needs and legitimate aspirations of other groups and even of the general welfare of the entire human family....

27. This Council lays stress on reverence for the human person. Each and all must consider every one of their neighbors without exception as another self, taking into account first of all their life and the means necessary to living it with dignity...whether that one be an old person abandoned by all, a foreign laborer unjustly looked down upon, a refugee, a child born of an unlawful union and wrongly suffering for a sin the child did not commit, or a hungry person who disturbs our conscience....Whatever is opposed to life itself, such as any type of murder, genocide, abortion, euthanasia, or willful self-destruction; whatever violates the integrity of the human person, such as mutilation, torments inflicted on body or mind, attempts to coerce the will itself; whatever insults human dignity, such as subhuman living conditions, arbitrary imprisonment, deportation, slavery, prostitution, the selling of women and children; as well as disgraceful working conditions, where women and men are treated as mere tools for profit rather than as free and responsible persons; all these things and others like them are infamies. While they poison human society, they do more harm to those who practice them than those who suffer from the injury. Moreover, they are a supreme dishonor to the Creator....

29. It must still be regretted that fundamental personal rights are not yet being universally honored. Such is the case of a woman who is denied the right and freedom to choose a husband, to embrace a state of life, or to acquire an education or cultural benefits equal to those recognized for men....Excessive economic and social differences between the members of the one human family or population groups cause scandal and militate against social justice, equity, and the dignity of the human person as well as social and international peace....

The Incarnate Word and Human Solidarity

32. God did not create women and men for life in isolation, but for the formation of social unity. So also "it has pleased God to make women and men holy and save them not merely as individuals

without any mutual bonds but by making them into a people, who acknowledge him in truth and serve him in holiness."[1] ...

This communitarian character is developed and consummated in the work of Jesus Christ. For the Word made flesh willed to share in the human fellowship. He was present at the wedding of Cana, visited the house of Zacchaeus, ate with publicans and sinners. He revealed the love of the Father and the sublime vocation of the human person in terms of the most common social realities and by making use of the speech and the imagery of plain everyday life. Willingly obeying the laws of his country, he sanctified those human ties, especially family ones from which social relationships arise. He chose to lead the life proper to an artisan of his time and place.

In his preaching he clearly taught the sons and daughters of God to treat one another as brothers and sisters. In his prayers he pleaded that all his disciples might be "one." Indeed, as the Redeemer of all, he offered himself for all even to the point of death. "Greater love than this no one has than that one lay down one's life for one's friends" (Jn. 15:13). He commanded his apostles to preach to all peoples the Gospel message so that the human race might become the family of God in which the fullness of the law would be love.

Human Activity throughout the World

34. Far from thinking that works produced by the human's own talent and energy are in opposition to God's power and that the rational creature exists as a kind of rival to the Creator, Christians are convinced that the triumphs of the human race are a sign of God's greatness and the flowering of his own ineffable design. The greater human power becomes, the farther human individual and community responsibility extends....

35. Just as human activity proceeds from the human person, so it is ordered toward the human person. For when women and men work they not only change things and society, they develop them-

---

1. Second Vatican Council, Dogmatic Constitution concerning Church, 9.

selves as well. They learn much, they cultivate their resources, they go outside themselves and beyond themselves. Rightly understood, this kind of growth is of greater value than any external riches which can be garnered. Women and men are more precious for what they are than for what they have. Similarly, all that women and men do to obtain greater justice, wider brother- and sisterhood, and a more humane ordering of social relationships has greater worth than technical advances. For these advances can supply the material for human progress but of themselves alone they can never actually bring it about.

Hence the norm of human activity is this: that in accord with the divine plan and will, it should harmonize with the genuine good of the human race and allow women and men as individuals and as members of society to pursue their total vocation and fulfill it....

Human Activity Finds Perfection in the Paschal Mystery

38. God's Word, through whom all things were made, was himself made flesh and dwelt on the earth of women and men. Thus he entered the world's history as a perfect man, taking that history up into himself and summarizing it. He himself revealed to us that "God is love" (1 Jn. 4:8). At the same time he taught us that the new command of love was the basic law of human perfection and hence of the world's transformation.

To those, therefore, who believe in divine love, he gives assurance that the way of love lies open to all and that the effort to establish a universal brother- and sisterhood is not a hopeless one. He cautions them at the same time that this love is not something to be reserved for important matters, but must be pursued chiefly in the ordinary circumstances of life.

Undergoing death itself for all of us sinners, he taught us by example that we too must shoulder that cross which the world and the flesh inflict upon those who search after peace and justice. Appointed Lord by his resurrection and given plenary power in heaven and on earth, Christ now works in the hearts of women and men through the power of his Spirit, arousing not only a desire for the age to come but animating, purifying, and strengthening those generous longings by which the human family strives to make its life more human and to use the whole earth to this end....

39. We do not know the time for the consummation of the earth and of humanity. Nor do we know how all things will be transformed. As deformed by sin, the shape of this world will pass away. But we are taught that God is preparing a new dwelling place and a new earth where justice will abide and whose blessedness will answer and surpass all the longings for peace which spring up in the human heart. Then, with death overcome, the daughters and sons of God will be raised up in Christ. What was sown in weakness and corruption will be clothed with incorruptibility.

The Role of the Church in the Modern World

40. The Church has a saving and an eschatological purpose which can be fully attained only in the future world. But the Church is present here in this world. It is composed of women and men, members of the earthly city. These are called to form God's family during this present time and to keep it growing until the Lord returns....

43. Often enough the Christian view of things will itself suggest some specific solution in certain circumstances. Yet it happens rather frequently, and legitimately so, that with equal sincerity some of the faithful will disagree with others on a given matter. Even against the intention of their proponents, however, solutions proposed on one side or another may be easily confused by many people with the Gospel message. Hence it is necessary for people to remember that none are allowed in such situations to appropriate the Church's authority for their opinion. They should always try to enlighten one another through honest discussion, preserving mutual charity and caring above all for the common good.

44. The Church knows how richly it has profited by the history and development of humanity.... Thanks to the experience of past ages, the progress of the sciences, and the treasures hidden in the

various forms of human culture, the nature of the human person itself is more clearly revealed and new roads to truth are opened. These benefits profit the Church, too. For, from the beginning of its history, it has learned to express the message of Christ with the help of the ideas and terminology of various peoples and has tried to clarify it with the wisdom of philosophers, too.

The Church's aim has been to set forth the Gospel in a way that it can be grasped by all as well as satisfy the needs of the learned insofar as such is possible. This accommodated preaching of the revealed Word ought to remain the law of all evangelization. For thus each nation develops the ability to express Christ's message in its own way. At the same time, a living exchange is fostered between the Church and the diverse cultures of the peoples.

To promote such an exchange, the Church requires special help, particularly in our day when things are changing very rapidly and the ways of thinking are exceedingly various. It must rely on those who live in the world, are versed in different institutions and specialties, and grasp their innermost significance in the eyes of both believers and unbelievers. With the help of Holy Spirit it is the task of the entire People of God, especially pastors and theologians, to hear, distinguish, and interpret the many voices of our age and to judge them in the light of the divine Word. In this way revealed truth can always be more deeply penetrated, better understood, and set forth to greater advantage....

Christ, the Alpha and the Omega

45. God's Word, by whom all things were made, was himself made flesh so that as perfect human he might save all women and men and sum up all things in himself. The Lord is the goal of human history, the focal point of the longings of history and of civilization, the center of the human race, the joy of every heart, and the answer to all its yearnings. He it is whom the Father raised from the dead, lifted on high, and stationed at his right hand, making him judge of the living and the dead. Enlivened and united in his Spirit, we journey toward the consummation of human history, one which fully

accords with the counsel of God's love: "To re-establish all things in Christ, both those in the heavens and those on the earth" (Eph. 1:10).

The Lord himself speaks: "Behold I come quickly! And my reward is with me to render to each according to one's works. I am the Alpha and the Omega, the first and the last, the beginning and the end" (Rev. 22:12–13).

With the foundation laid out in part one and building upon it, the fathers go on in the second part of the constitution to a consideration of "a number of particularly urgent needs characterizing the present age...in the light of the Gospel and of human experience." They settled on a half dozen or so, woven into five chapters.

The first chapter turned its attention to marriage and the family. As in most of these chapters, there is not much that is new, but there is a precise setting forth of some of the rich teaching of the Church on the matter. From a very practical point of view, but not only from that point of view, what is perhaps most significant in this first chapter is what is not said. It could be looked at as something of a historical accident but that would be selling it short indeed. It is rather a working of the Providence that mysteriously guided the Council in all. At the time the Council fathers came to study this matter, the pope had summoned a large group of experts to advise him on the matter of birth control. In view of this consultation the pope reserved the discernment of this matter to himself. Thus here, and in the later section on population, the Council makes no decision on the extent to which couples can use modern technology in controlling pregnancies. While pointing out the teaching authority of the Church in the matter they leave the question wide open:

Human beings should be judiciously informed of scientific advances in the exploration of methods by which couples can be helped in arranging the number of their children. The reliability of these methods should be adequately proven and their harmony with the moral order should be clear. (87)

It did cause a great upset in the Church, to say the least, when Pope Paul judged in conscience that he could not follow the advice that the majority of his commission gave him in regard to the matter. There, of course, had been a great deal of evolution in regards to marital sex since the days St. Augustine's teaching inspired the teaching of the magisterium: married couples were to engage in intercourse only for procreation and were to hold back as much as they could from any enjoyment of it or any passion. The so-called natural method of rhythm, which Pius XI condemned and Pius XII allowed was now being strongly advocated as a way, if not *the* way, to exercise responsible marital chastity. The next step to many seemed to be for couples to use the fruits of modern technology to have greater freedom in their expression of marital love along with greater facility and sureness in fulfilling their obligation to responsible procreation.

What is hurting more, though, at this time, is the seeming unwillingness of many in the teaching magisterium to enter into open dialogue with the many faithful Catholic couples who feel they have something to say "in the light of the Gospel and human experience" in regards to this matter that touches their lives so deeply. If the teaching leadership of the Church does not in fact live an open dialogical stance — which the Council professes it holds — in regards to its own devout members, how will the separated brothers and sisters, the believers of other faiths, and non-believers place any trust in the Church as a dialogue partner. Moreover, this closedness has forced many good Catholics to painfully make their own decisions in conscience. And doing this, unfortunately, instead of enhancing the personal responsibility of the couple as believing members of the Church, has, all too often, undermined the effective presence of the teaching Church in the couples' lives and subsequently in the lives of their offspring. Indeed, what the fathers say in their Conclusion to this document applies here: the matter will have to be further pursued and amplified since it deals with matters in a constant state of development.

Fostering the Nobility of Marriage and the Family

47. The well-being of the individual person and of the human and Christian society is intimately linked with the healthy condition of that community produced by marriage and family....

48. The intimate partnership of married life and love has been established by the Creator and qualified by his laws. It is rooted in the conjugal covenant of irrevocable personal consent. Hence, by that human act whereby couples mutually give themselves and accept each other, a relationship arises which by divine will is a lasting one. Society also sees it this way. For the good of the couple and their offspring as well as of society, the existence of this sacred bond no longer depends on human decisions alone.... Marriage and conjugal love are by their nature ordained toward the begetting and educating of children....

50. Hence, while not making the other purposes of matrimony of less account, the true practice of conjugal love and the whole meaning of the family life which results from it have this aim: that the couple be ready with courageous hearts to cooperate with the love of the Creator and the Savior, who through them will enlarge and enrich his own family day by day.

Parents should regard as their proper mission the task of transmitting human life and educating those to whom it has been transmitted. They should realize that they are thereby cooperators with the love of God the Creator and are, so to speak, the interpreters of that love. Thus they will fulfill their task with human and Christian responsibility. With docile reverence toward God they will come to the right decision by common counsel and effort.

They will thoughtfully take into account both their own welfare and that of their children, those already born and those which may be foreseen. For this accounting they will reckon with both the material and the spiritual conditions of the times as well as of their state in life. Finally, they will consult the interests of the family group, of temporal society, and of the Church itself.

The parents themselves should ultimately make this judgment in the sight of God. But in their manner of acting, couples should be aware that they cannot proceed arbitrarily. They must always be governed according to a conscience dutifully conformed to the divine law itself and should be submissive toward the Magisterium of the Church, which interprets that law in the light of the Gospel. That divine law reveals and protects the integral meaning of conjugal love and impels it toward a truly human fulfillment. . . .

51. The Council realizes that certain modern conditions often keep couples from arranging their married lives harmoniously, and thus they find themselves in circumstances where at least temporarily the size of their families should not be increased. As a result the faithful exercise of love and the full intimacy of their lives are hard to maintain. But where the intimacy of married life is broken off it is not rare for its faithfulness to be imperiled and its quality of fruitfulness ruined. . . . When there is question of harmonizing conjugal love with the responsible transmission of life, the moral aspect of any procedure does not depend solely on sincere intentions or on an evaluation of motives. It must be determined by objective standards. Those based on the nature of human persons and their acts preserve the full sense of mutual self-giving and human procreation in the context of true love. Such a goal cannot be achieved unless the virtue of conjugal chastity is sincerely practiced. Relying on these principles, sons and daughters of the Church may not undertake methods of regulating procreation which are found blameworthy by the teaching authority of the Church in its unfolding of the divine law. . . .

52. Those who are skilled in sciences, notably medical, biological, social, and psychological, can considerably advance the welfare of marriage and the family, along with peace of conscience, if by

pooling their efforts they labor to explain more thoroughly the various conditions favoring a proper regulation of births.

The Proper Development of Culture

The second chapter is significant in the way it calls us to a deeper, richer, and fuller consideration of culture, which it defines as

...all those factors by which women and men refine and develop their manifold spiritual and corporal qualities: their effort to bring the world itself under their control by their knowledge and their labor; rendering social life more human both within the family and in the civic community by improving customs and institutions; expressing, communicating, and conserving in their works great spiritual experiences and desires throughout the course of time so that these may be of advantage to the progress of many, even of the whole human family. (53)

The Council points to the birth of a "new humanism," one in which "human persons are defined first of all by their responsibility toward their sisters and brothers and toward history." In the rushing currents of technological advance how, the Council asks, "can women and men preserve the ability to contemplate and to wonder, from whence comes wisdom?" "The human spirit," it argues, "must be cultivated in such a way that there results a growth in its ability to wonder, to understand, to contemplate, to make personal judgments, and to develop a religious, moral, and social sense." The answers are not readily at hand. "For recent studies and findings of science, history, and philosophy raise new questions which influence life and demand new theological investigation." In the meantime much needs to be done to give every human person the leisure and spaciousness in their lives out of which culture can grow and be enjoyed.

The Council also champions the role of freedom in the development of culture, while calling for a new appreciation of the sciences in the pastoral mission of the Church.

59. Because it flows immediately from the spiritual and social nature of women and men, culture has constant need of a just freedom if it is to develop. It also needs the legitimate possibility of exercising its independence according to its own principles. Rightly, therefore, it demands respect and enjoys a certain inviolability, at least as long as the rights of the individual and of the community, whether particular or universal, are preserved within the context of the common good....

There are "two orders of knowledge," which are distinct, namely, faith and reason. The Church does not indeed forbid that "when the human arts and sciences are practiced they use their own principles and their proper method, each in its own domain." Hence, "acknowledging this just liberty," this Synod affirms the legitimate autonomy of human culture and especially of the sciences....[2]

All these considerations demand also that within the limits of morality and the general welfare women and men be free to search for the truth, voice their minds and publicize them, practice any art they choose, and finally have appropriate access to information about public affairs. It is not the function of public authority to determine what the proper characteristics of the forms of human culture should be. It should rather foster the conditions and the means which are capable of promoting cultural life among all citizens, even within the minorities of a nation....

62. Recent studies and findings of science, history, and philosophy raise new questions which influence life and demand new theological investigation. While adhering to the methods and requirements proper to theology, theologians are to seek continually for more suitable ways of communicating doctrine to the women and men of their times. For the deposit of faith or revealed truths is one thing; the manner in which they are formulated, safeguarding

---

2. First Vatican Council, *Constitution on the Catholic Faith*, Denzinger 1795 and 1799.

always their meaning and significance, is another. In pastoral care appropriate use must be made not only of theological principles but also of the findings of the secular sciences, especially of psychology and sociology. Thus the faithful can be brought to live the faith in a more thorough and mature way.

Literature and the arts are also in their own way of great importance to the life of the Church. For they strive to probe the unique nature of human persons, their problems, and their experiences as they struggle to know and perfect both themselves and the world. These are preoccupied with revealing women and men's place in history and in the world, with illustrating their miseries and joys, their needs and strengths, and with foreshadowing a better life for them. Thus these are able to elevate human life as it is expressed in manifold forms in different times and places. Efforts must therefore be made so that those who exercise these arts can feel that the Church gives recognition to them in their activities and so that enjoying a proper freedom they can establish smoother relations with the Christian community. Let the Church also acknowledge new forms of art which are adapted to our age and are in keeping with the characteristics of various nations and regions. Adjusted in their mode of expression and conformed to liturgical requirements, they may be introduced into the sanctuary when they raise the mind to God.

Socio-Economic Life

The next chapter explores the manifold challenges that lie in the socio-economic life of the modern world within the political community. As challenges are catalogued, principles, enlightened by faith and Revelation, are put forth, the beginning of the Church's cooperation with the secular world in facing these challenges. Needless to say, it is a daunting task that lies ahead for us all. The strong personalist philosophy of Pope John Paul II resonates with the Council fathers here as they strongly insist that persons must come first.

63. Modern economy is marked by women and men's increasing domination of nature, by closer and more intense relationships between citizens, groups, and countries and by their mutual dependence, and by more frequent intervention on the part of government. At the same time progress in the methods of production and in the exchange of goods and services has made the economy an apt instrument for meeting the intensified needs of the human family more successfully.

Reasons for anxiety, however, are not lacking. Many people, especially in economically advanced areas, seem to be hypnotized, as it were, by economics so that almost their entire personal and social life is permeated with a certain economic outlook. These people can be found both in nations which favor a collective economy as well as in others.

Again, we are at a moment in history when the development of economic life could diminish social inequalities if that development were guided and coordinated in a reasonable and human way. Yet all too often it serves only to intensify the inequalities. In some places it even results in a decline in the social status of the weak and in contempt for the poor.

While an enormous mass of people still lack the absolute necessities of life, some even in less advanced countries live sumptuously or squander wealth.... A similar lack of economic and social balance is to be noted between agriculture, industry, and the services and also between different parts of one and the same country. The contrast between the economically more advanced countries and other countries is becoming more serious day by day and the very peace of the world can be jeopardized in consequence....

64. The fundamental purpose of productivity must not be the mere multiplication of products. It must not be profit or domination. Rather, it must be the service of women and men and indeed of the whole of the human person, viewed in terms of their material needs and the demands of their intellectual, moral, spiritual, and religious life....

65. Economic development must be kept under the control of humankind. It must not be left to the sole judgment of a few

women and men or groups possessing excessive power or of the political community alone or of certain especially powerful nations. It is proper, on the contrary, that at every level the largest possible number of people have an active share in directing that development....

67. Human labor which is expended in the production and exchange of goods or in the performance of economic services is superior to the other elements of economic life.... The entire process of productive work, therefore, must be adapted to the needs of persons and to the requirements of their lives, above all their domestic life....

68. In economic enterprises it is persons who work together, that is, free and independent human beings created to the image of God. Therefore the active participation of everyone in the running of an enterprise should be promoted.... Among the basic rights of the human person must be counted the right of freely founding labor unions.... Even in present-day circumstances the strike can still be a necessary though ultimate means for the defense of the workers' own rights and the fulfillment of their just demands. As soon as possible, however, ways should be sought to resume negotiations and the discussion of reconciliation....

69. For the rest, the right to have a share of earthly goods sufficient for oneself and one's family belongs to everyone. The Fathers and doctors of the Church held this view, teaching that women and men are obliged to come to the relief of the poor and to do so not merely out of their superfluous goods. If a person is in extreme necessity that person has the right to take from the riches of others what that person needs....

70. The investment of goods should be directed toward providing employment and sufficient income for the people of today and of the future....

71. Ownership and other forms of private control over material goods contribute to the expression of personality. Moreover, they furnish women and men with an occasion for exercising their role in society and in the economy. Hence it is very important to facilitate the access of both individuals and communities to

some control over material goods. Private ownership or some other kind of dominion over material goods provides everyone with a wholly necessary area of independence and should be regarded as an extension of human freedom. Finally since it adds incentives for carrying on one's function and duty, it contributes a kind of prerequisite for civil liberties....

The right of private control, however, is not opposed to the right inherent in various forms of public ownership. Still goods can be transferred to the public domain only by the competent authority according to the demands and within the limits of the common good, and with fair compensation....

The Life of the Political Community

74. Political community exists for that common good in which the community finds its full justification and meaning and from which it derives its pristine and proper right. The common good embraces the sum of those conditions of social life by which individuals, families, and groups can achieve their own fulfillment in a relatively thorough and ready way.

Many different people go to make up the political community, and these can lawfully incline toward diverse ways of doing things. If the political community is not to be torn to pieces as each follows one's own viewpoint, authority is needed. This authority must dispose the energies of the whole citizenry toward the common good, not mechanically or despotically, but primarily as a moral force which depends on freedom and the conscientious discharge of the burdens of any office which has been undertaken.

It is therefore obvious that the political community and public authority are based on human nature and hence belong to an order of things divinely foreordained. At the same time the choice of government and the method of selecting leaders is left to the free will of citizens....

Where public authority oversteps its competence and oppresses the people, the people should nonetheless obey to the extent that the objective common good demands. Still it is lawful for them to defend their own rights and those of their fellow citizens against any abuse of this authority, provided that in so doing they observe the limits imposed by natural law and the Gospel....

75. It is in full accord with human nature that juridical-political structures should with ever better success and without any discrimination afford all their citizens the chance to participate freely and actively in establishing the constitutional bases of the political community, governing the state, determining the scope and purpose of various institutions, and choosing leaders. Let all citizens be mindful of their simultaneous right and duty to vote freely in the interest of advancing the common good....

76. The role and competence of the Church being what it is, it must in no way be confused with the political community nor bound to any political system. For it is a sign and a safeguard of the transcendence of the human person.

In their proper spheres, the political community and the Church are mutually independent and self-governing. Yet by a different title each serves the personal and social vocation of the same human beings. This service can be more effectively rendered for the good of all if each works more for wholesome mutual cooperation in accord with the circumstances of time and place....

But it is always and everywhere legitimate for the Church to preach the faith with true freedom, to teach its social doctrine, and to discharge its duty among women and men without hindrance. It also has the right to pass moral judgments, even on matters touching the political order, whenever basic personal rights or the salvation of souls make such judgments necessary.

Peace and the Promotion of a Community of Nations

In the last chapter, where we look at fostering peace and the promotion of a community of nations, we meet a great disappointment. We would have wanted the fathers to re-echo Pope Paul's resounding cry at the United Nations: "No more war!" They did ask that his impassioned plea be read into the records of the Council. But nowhere in the documents of the Council is the politics of compromise so evident as here. While the fathers decry the arms race and especially what it has been doing to the poor of the world, they yet espouse a just war theory that demands ever-developing armaments. One wonders, could such a blatant and painful contradiction have been missed by the fathers, could it have been truly intended by the Spirit? Or was a blindness, induced by connections with the power and money of this world, so great that it impeded the reception of the light and grace of the Spirit? There was no infallibility at work here, and the moral guidance is certainly suspect. The Gospel mandate, lived so courageously by the Father of the Indian nation, is left aside by these men so solemnly commissioned to proclaim the Gospel to all nations, even big, powerful nations like the United States, so wedded to a war economy. A rather begrudging place is given to the conscience of the man or woman of peace: "It seems right that the laws make humane provisions...." A more generous commendation is given to those who courageously stood against the crimes of war: "The courage of those who openly and fearlessly resist men or women who issue such commands merits supreme commendation."

78. Peace is not merely the absence of war.... Peace results from that harmony built into human society by its divine Founder and actualized by women and men as they thirst after ever greater justice.

The common good of women and men is in its basic sense determined by the eternal law. Still the concrete demands of this common good are constantly changing as time goes on. Hence peace is never attained once and for all but must be built up ceaselessly. Moreover, since the human will is unsteady and wounded by sin the achievement of peace requires that all persons constantly master their passions and that lawful authority keep vigilant.

But such is not enough. This peace cannot be obtained on earth unless personal values are safeguarded and women and men freely and trustingly share with one another the riches of their inner spirits and their talents. A firm determination to respect other individuals and peoples and their dignity as well as the serious practice of sister- and brotherhood are absolutely necessary for the establishment of peace. Peace is the fruit of a love which goes beyond what justice can give us....

80. Any act of war aimed indiscriminately at the destruction of entire cities or of extensive areas along with their population is a crime against God and the human person. It merits unequivocal and unhesitating condemnation....

81. Men and women should be convinced that the arms race in which so many countries are engaged is not a safe way to preserve a steady peace. Nor is the so-called balance resulting from this race a sure and authentic peace. Rather than being eliminated, the causes of war threaten to grow gradually stronger. While extravagant sums are being spent for the furnishing of ever new weapons, an adequate remedy cannot be provided for the multiple miseries afflicting the whole modern world....Therefore it must be said again: the arms race is an utterly treacherous trap for humanity and one which injures the poor to an intolerable degree....

82. It is our clear duty then to strain every muscle as we work for the time when all war can be completely outlawed by international consent....

Men and women should take heed not to entrust themselves only to the efforts of others while remaining careless about their own attitudes. For government officials, who must simultaneously guarantee the good of their own people and promote the universal good, depend on public opinion and feeling to the greatest possible extent. It does them no good to work at building peace so long as feelings of hostility, contempt, and distrust as well as racial hatred and unbending ideologies continue to divide individuals and place them in opposing camps....

88. Some nations with a majority of citizens who are counted as Christians have an abundance of this world's goods while others are

deprived of the necessities of life and are tormented with hunger, disease, and every kind of misery. This situation must not be allowed to continue to the scandal of humanity. For the spirit of poverty and of charity are the glory and authentication of the Church of Christ....As was the ancient custom of the Church, they should meet this obligation out of the substance of their goods and not only out of what is superfluous.

The Pastoral Constitution concerning Church in the Modern World, while an ending and crowning of the labors of the fathers gathered in Council, is yet a beginning, a good beginning to the work of the Council in the world. If the fathers and all their worthy successors could but live the open dialogical stance set forth here and inculcate this into the lives of all the faithful, what a strongly united and powerfully evangelical Church we would be in the modern world.

Such a mission requires in the first place that we foster within the Church itself mutual esteem, reverence, and harmony through the full recognition of lawful diversity. Thus all those who compose the one People of God, both pastors and the general faithful, can engage in dialogue with ever abounding fruitfulness. For the bonds which unite the faithful are mightier than anything which divides them. So let there be unity in what is necessary, freedom in what is questionable, and charity in all. (92)

If the modern world saw this truly present among us it would begin to listen, to be willing to enter into honest conversation with us. And as we work together to create a world more in harmony with the greatest of human aspirations, a kinship would develop that might blossom into a communion. The fathers of the Council spent more than one page in the document detailing what the Church can learn from the world. They made it clear that we do not have all the answers or ready-made answers. We do have a supreme contribution to bring to this dialogue — and dialogue may well be the way to proclaim the Gospel to all nations today. But it is not a one-way street. We must welcome atheists and the faithful of other religions as men and women who rightly believe they have something to teach the Church. That is the difficult and profound change of heart — *metanoia* — to which the Spirit calls us and tells us is the way we can hope to be effectively present to the world today.

6

Some More Corollaries

As the Church looks out upon the modern world, its gaze first lights on fellow believers, not just those who are clearly members of the People of God in virtue of a common baptism. But those who share a faith that in some way reaches beyond the material world for answers.

DECLARATION CONCERNING THE RELATIONSHIP OF THE CHURCH TO NON-CHRISTIAN RELIGIONS

In the Declaration concerning the Relationship of the Church to Non-Christian Religions the fathers marshal those questions that are most common to thinking men and women: What is a human person? What is the meaning and the purpose of our life? What is goodness and what is sin? What gives rise to our sorrows and to what intent? Where lies the path to true happiness? What is the truth about death, judgment, and retribution beyond the grave? What, finally, is that ultimate and unutterable mystery that engulfs our being from where we take our rise and whither our journey leads us?

In the spirit of frank and honest dialogue, the fathers

then set forth the Church's convictions in regard to these questions. Ultimately Christ is the answer.

At the same time the fathers of the Council wanted to express their profound respect for others who, often times at great personal cost, have found answers elsewhere and are living them. But they went a good bit further. They not only exhort all Christians to follow the Council's example in honoring these believers, but they urge them to act positively to preserve and even promote all that is good in other religions: Hinduism, Buddhism, and other world religions. They call for dialogue and for collaboration. This is light years away from the time when it was considered almost a mortal sin for a Catholic to put a foot inside a Protestant church. Many Christians can bear witness to the benefit that has accrued to them because of this new openness, how they have come to discover the contemplative richness of their own Christian heritage through contact with other traditions that have better preserved in practice the contemplative dimension of life so desperately needed in our frenetic times.

The fathers show deep respect and reverence toward Islam, acknowledging that both sides, Moslem and Christian, have things to forgive and forget as we move forward to a new collaboration for the benefit of humankind. The fathers bring out some of the many things we cherish in common. While they note that Moslems honor Jesus at least as a prophet and honor his virgin Mother, there is unfortunately no indication of any Christian reverence for their Prophet. Dialogue is not explicitly encouraged here, only humane collaboration. There seems to be room for more growth in our response to the followers of Mohammed.

The Declaration concerning the Relationship of the Church to Non-Christian Religions is a very short document, and its content would seem to be hardly controversial. But it received more publicity than any other Council doc-

ument and evoked the most heated controversy outside the
walls of St. Peter's. This was due in part to this short, respectful passage on Islam, but much more to the longer and
much more complicated text concerning our Jewish sisters
and brothers. It was difficult for peoples whose ethnic religion was so much one with their political situation to divorce
the pronouncements of the Council from the political stand
of the papal government of the Vatican. In any case the fathers of the Council could not ignore the fact that whatever
they had to say as a large international body representing
close to a billion people would have repercussions outside of
Church circles. The Jewish people, though in large part secularized, were trying to establish a homeland and experienced
themselves as greatly threatened by the Islamic nations. Any
statement from the Council that could be interpreted as fa-
vorable to the Arabs or condemnatory toward the Jews was
deeply resented.

There are many deep wounds from the past. History sadly
recounts terrible persecutions of the Jewish people. While the
most recent and most deadly, which annihilated a good third
of the Jewish people, was perpetrated by a godless dictator-
ship that was as anti-Christian as it was anti-Jewish, the Jews
could nonetheless point a blaming finger at the Christians for
the precedents that inspired and were used in some ways to
justify this attempted genocide.

The fathers of the Council could not rewrite history. There
were some Jews responsible in their own way for the death of
our Lord and Founder. But the fathers decried the false theology that was fabricated on the basis of this historical fact.
The basic Christian reality that our Lord came and suffered
and died because of the sins of us all cannot be forgotten.
None can legitimately shift the blame on a particular people;
we are all responsible for his redeeming passion and death.
And we are all meant to benefit by it.

Many Jewish people will probably never be satisfied with the carefully nuanced statements of the Council fathers. But all will have to hear the loud and clear denunciation of any and all prejudice and persecution and the fathers' special pain and censure in regard to what our Jewish sisters and brothers have suffered. As we see intolerance on the rise again, we can only hope that these very clear words of the Council will inspire in more Christians the courage to stand by not only the Jewish people but any other people in their time of persecution. This necessarily includes our Palestinian brothers and sisters when they suffer at the hands of the Jews. It is a strange and sad fact that the abused so often become in their turn the abusers. The Council says little about the sufferings of persecuted Christians, but we too must forgive from our hearts and take care that we do not in turn become persecutors. In Christlike fashion we should ever turn the other cheek.

Most of us deem ourselves, and probably quite rightly, as being too civilized to engage in persecution. Yet it was the silent complicity of the masses and the petty jealousies and prejudices of many that made it possible for a few savages to carry out their atrocities. We must not only hear the Council's strong denunciation of hatred and persecution, but we need to foster in our own consciousness the profound spirit of reverence that they seek to inculcate in this declaration. The Church has rightly accorded its highest honors to Maximilian Kolbe for laying down his life for a fellow Christian, but we have yet to honor in a similar fashion any of those who courageously sacrificed themselves for their Jewish brothers and sisters. Why is this?

It is worth noting that the secretariat established to implement and carry forward the thrust of this declaration has changed its name from the Secretariat for Non-Christians to the Secretariat for World Religions. This more positive and less self-centered nomenclature gives witness to the fact that there continues to be a growth in our sensitivity in our outreach to our fellow humans of different persuasions. The declaration is being effective in practice.

In the face of the Church's reverence for the faith of women and men of other religions and for the good will of secular humanists and its espousal of a dialogical attitude toward all, what is to become of our traditional missionary outreach?

DECREE CONCERNING THE CHURCH'S MISSIONARY ACTIVITY

The Council's Decree concerning the Church's Missionary Activity seeks to answer this question as it sets missionary activity in a new Church and world context. It does this most successfully in regard to the new ecumenical attitude of the Church. Honor is shown to all the baptized, and collaboration is espoused. The term "missions" in this document is tightly defined: it is a going forth to peoples or groups who do not yet believe in Christ. To some extent the old Eastern-dominated idea of missionary outreach prevails. Not completely, however. Mission Churches are called upon to join in the effort. Inculturation is strongly affirmed. Dialogue with non-Christians is again endorsed. And the mission Church is welcomed to take its place within the universal Church. It is also encouraged to find its own contemplative heart:

Worthy of special mention are the various projects aimed at helping the contemplative life take root. There are those who while retaining the essential elements of monastic life are bent on implanting the very rich traditions of their own order. Others are returning to simpler forms of ancient monasticism. But all are striving to work

out a genuine adaptation to local conditions. For the contemplative life belongs to the fullness of the Church's presence and should
therefore be everywhere established. (18)

The fathers repeatedly remind us that the whole Church is
missionary, that all are called to missionary activity. It is the
Church's journey from the Incarnation and Pentecost to the
eschaton. Yet the document is heavy on structures, organiza-
tion, and hierarchy. Individual free initiative is not endorsed.
It speaks primarily to missionaries and mission Churches and
develops little in regard to how the average Christian in the
established Churches can participate. A personal internal renewal, an informed consciousness, a caring are called for,
but there is little said about personal missionary activity. I
would have liked to see more encouragement of parents to
prepare their sons and daughters to go forth and share the
Good News. I would have liked to see all youth encouraged
to give a year or two or more of their lives in missionary activity, following the inspiring example of some of the
other Christian Churches. If the whole Church is missionary, why are not all called to personal active participation in
mission?

This was one of the last documents of the Council I reread
and meditated upon as I prepared this volume. As I did I
found a certain anger welling up within me, especially as I
read the section on the preparation of priests in the mission
Churches. As I read the program the bishops laid down here
for these seminarians I asked myself: How many of these
bishops honestly had any intention or expectation of making it possible for their seminarians to fulfill these directives?
It would be impossible for any man to accomplish what is
laid out here in four, six, or even eight years. The end result
of this idealistic description of preparation for the ministry
can only result in the young priest, who already is painfully

conscious of his inadequacies, being further depressed because of the inadequacy of his preparation, at least by the standards of this unrealistic program. This kind of unrealistic idealism is repeatedly found in the decrees of the Council in regards to the activities of the bishops themselves, of the priests, and of the laity. Instead of inspiring the reader it depresses.

It is perhaps not so much what is said as the way in which it is said. If it were stated as being an expression of ideals, goals, and aspirations, it might inspire effort to press toward an increasing realization. But when the very men who are going to be most responsible for the decrees' realization set their idealistic programs forth as something that all are to carry out, it makes me wonder about their honesty and sincerity. Were they caught up and lost in a flurry of rhetoric as in the closing words of this decree where they speak of themselves as being "afire" with love toward men. I do not remember seeing too many burning bishops at the Council. There are passages where the decrees of the Council are very sincere and humble, but more often they are lacking in that direct simplicity that would have been more inspiring and effective.

This decree on missionary activity has some sections that are closely inspired by the Scriptures and are themselves inspiring. The urgent command of the Master to go forth and bring the Good News to all still has its power. In giving that command voice in the context of the renewing Church, the decree does not depart from the basic thrust of the Council with its reverence for the modern world. Its implementation will need to be carefully informed with the affirmations and principles of the Declaration concerning the Relationship of the Church to Non-Christian Religions.

THE DECLARATION CONCERNING
CHRISTIAN EDUCATION

Like the Decree concerning the Instruments of Social Communication, the Declaration concerning Christian Education touches on a matter of greatest importance, yet does so in a rather prosaic and uninspiring way. It does not very effectively face the challenge that addresses the Church in societies where a completely secularized government, which is often hostile to religion in varying degrees, has taken over education. How does a Christian spirit inform a decade or two of godless education so that the end result is a cultured Christian? When we close our parish schools and Catholic high schools do we throw in the towel on Christian education? When understood in the context of the principles of the Pastoral Constitution concerning Church in the Modern World, the emphasis on the home and family and on the role of parents is undoubtedly giving significant direction for the future. There is much room for development here.

7

In Freedom: More Than a Corollary

Development is certainly one of the reasons why the very short Declaration concerning Religious Freedom is important. It is important also because of what it has to say in regard to freedom. And it is important because of the way it speaks. It presents a good example of the seriousness of the Church's intent to enter into dialogue with the modern world and with all humanity.

Like a good dialogue, the document begins with a listening. The fathers are listening to the world, to humanity, listening to its deepest aspirations: "A sense of the dignity of the human person has been impressing itself more and more deeply on the consciousness of contemporary persons. And the demand is increasingly made that women and men should act on their own judgment, enjoying and making use of a responsible freedom, not driven by coercion.... The demand is also made that there should be set constitutional limits to the powers of government in order that there may be no encroachment on the rightful freedom of the person and of associations." It goes on to resonate its agreement with this deep-seated demand for freedom: "This Vatican Synod [note:

it is no longer "this Most Holy Council" as it was in the first documents the Council set forth, but now simply "this Vatican Synod"] takes careful note of these desires in the minds of women and men ... to declare them to be greatly in accord with truth and justice."

As a good dialogical partner, the Council goes on to state clearly where it itself stands, the position it holds as it comes to the conversation: "This Synod professes its belief that God himself has made known to humankind the way in which women and men are to serve him and thus be saved in Christ and come to blessedness. We believe that this one true religion subsists in the catholic and apostolic Church to which the Lord Jesus committed the duty of spreading it abroad among all" (1).

The fathers then lock arms with their partners in dialogue and together with them proclaim to all the powers that be, governments and churches alike, their inviolable right to freedom in religious matters. "This Vatican Synod declares that the human person has a right to religious freedom. This freedom means that all women and men are to be immune from coercion on the part of individuals or social groups and of any human power in such wise that in matters of religion no one is to be forced to act in a manner contrary to his or her own beliefs. Nor is anyone to be restrained from acting in accordance with his or her own beliefs, whether privately or publicly, whether alone or in association with others ... " (2).

The Council in its Pastoral Constitution concerning Church in the Modern World and in its various decrees reaches out, seeking dialogue with the other Christian Churches, with the other religions, and with all humanity. In this declaration, which was one of its final words, it sought to set the context within which this dialogue can freely take place. While the fathers did not draw back from traditional Catholic teaching that "all women and men are bound to seek the truth, especially in what concerns God and his Church, and to embrace the truth they come to know and to hold it fast," they went on to affirm "that it is upon the human conscience that these obligations fall and exert their binding force. The truth cannot impose itself except by virtue of its own truth...."

Truth is to be sought in a manner proper to the dignity of the human person and that person's social nature. The inquiry is to be free, carried on with the aid of teaching or instruction, communication and dialogue. In the course of these, women and men explain to one another the truth they have discovered or think they have discovered in order thus to assist one another in the quest for truth. Moreover, as the truth is discovered it is by a personal assent that women and men are to adhere to it.... (3)

This is indeed a truly dialogical climate.

The conciliar debates around the formulation of this declaration on religious freedom elicited a lot of attention from the media. Where there is controversy, there the media is sure to be. But the controversy was in fact not really about these affirmations of human freedom. It was rather about another issue of great theological significance, an issue that was constantly at play just below the surface as the Council moved the Church into a new era, a new attitude, a new stance. And that was the question of the development of doctrine. No other document of the Council so explicitly faced the issue. The fathers, after stating the basic position — "the Church continually brings forth new things that are in harmony with the things that are old" — went on to declare their intention "to develop the doctrine of recent popes on the inviolable rights of the human person and on the constitutional order of society."

There was a long journey, which has yet to be fully explored, from the Syllabus of Errors of Pius IX and the affirmations of this declaration. Then, objective truth had all the rights, error was said to have no rights, full freedom was claimed exclusively for the Roman Catholic religion. Governments were to uphold the rights of truth. Now, the Church looks first to the human person. That person created by God with reason and freedom has the right to be free from coercion in exercising his or her freedom. Governments, which are established for the welfare of citizens, have the obligation not only to respect this freedom and hold back from any coercion but also to foster the freedom of individuals and the associations they form to exercise their rights. This is quite a development in outlook. And, being sanctioned by an ecumenical council, it sanctions the concept of the development of doctrine and opens the way for an ongoing development of all that the Council itself taught.

The freedom of the Spirit is once again fully recognized in the Church. It remains for us, the People of God, to fully claim and responsibly use the freedom that is ours. Unfortunately we are still all too prone to seek to use authority to clobber others and to find some pseudo security for ourselves. It takes a lot of courage, maturity, and energy to act as a truly free person. The early Fathers constantly pointed to *acedia*, an insidious spiritual sloth, as the vice that most saps the vitality and, therefore, the joy of Christian life. The Council, therefore, calls for personal development in this area as well as for education:

This Vatican Synod urges everyone, especially those who are charged with the task of educating others, to do their utmost to form women and men who will respect the moral order and be obedient to lawful authority. Let them form women and men who will be lovers of true freedom — women and men, in other words, who will come to decisions on their own judgment and in the light of truth, govern their activities with a sense of responsibility, and strive after what is true and right, willing always to join with others in cooperative effort. (8)

The Council's claim for religious freedom, which in the second part of the declaration is solidly grounded in the Revelation, is set forth in a very balanced and nuanced way. It is made primarily to governments, though propagators of religions are themselves warned to respect the rights of persons. "The protection and promotion of the inviolable rights of the human person rank among the essential duties of governments. Therefore government is to safeguard the religious freedom of all its citizens in an effective manner by just laws and by other appropriate means." It is not enough to have constitutional provisions; these exist in the constitution of the People's Republic of China and have supposedly been implemented by Proposition Nineteen and other laws, yet my brother monks have not only languished in communist prisons for decades but have even died in the midst of incredible suffering. The laws must in some way be made truly effective.

This claim is placed in the context of the common welfare, another notion that had undergone an evolution in the encyclicals of modern popes and even in the documents of the Council before arriving at the clear presentation we find here: "The common welfare of society consists in the entirety of those conditions of social life under which human beings enjoy the possibility of achieving their own perfection in a certain fullness and also with some relative ease." The rights of government are fully respected: "Provided the just requirements of public order are observed, religious bodies rightfully claim freedom...."

The right to religious freedom is exercised in human society; hence its exercise is subject to certain regulatory norms. In the use of all freedoms, the moral principle of personal and social responsibility is to be observed. In the exercise of their rights, individual women and men and social groups are bound by the moral law to have respect both for the rights of others and for their own duties toward others and for the common welfare of all. Women and men are to deal with their fellows in justice and civility. Furthermore, society has the right to defend itself against possible abuses committed on pretext of freedom of religion. (7)

Governments will in fact facilitate religious life and practice or at least hold back from undermining it or repressing it only if enough of their individual citizens are imbued with a sense of the dignity of the human person and the rights and duties that flow from that dignity. The Council has sought in the first part of this declaration (as in the Pastoral Constitution concerning Church in the Modern World) to affirm this dignity and its consequences in clear and simple terms that can easily be grasped and make sense even to those who themselves are not favored with religious faith but have a reverence for the human person.

The Second Vatican Council is far from complete. Few of us have even begun to absorb the fullness of its teaching and to implement its directives in our lives, in our Churches, and in our world. But with the Pastoral Constitution concerning Church in the Modern World and this Declaration concerning Religious Freedom the way is open for the work of the Second Vatican Council to move forward and continue to give direction to the People of God as they complete the second millennium of Christianity and move into the twenty-first century.

May the God and Father of all grant that the human family...may be brought by the grace of Christ and the power of Holy Spirit to the sublime and unending "freedom of the glory of the sons and daughters of God" (Rom. 8:21). (17)

Amen.

8

In the Light We Go Forward

In the course of a recent journey through China I visited the fabulously beautiful city of Guilin. There I found a small Catholic Church that had been built in 1936 by a missionary who is now, at age eighty-six, a Cistercian monk in the Trappist monastery on the Island of Lantau. I was greeted warmly; some of the oldest parishioners remembered their pastor, who was expelled from China in 1953. The young pastor, who had been a priest but three years, could speak no English and my Mandarin is limited to say the very least. He reached up and took down from his shelf of a dozen or so books a handsome volume, almost folio in size and beautifully bound, and laid it out before me. To my amazement, it was a copy of the 1983 *Code of Canon Law,* with the Latin text on one page, the Chinese translation on the facing page. We then proceeded to carry on a conversation: he pointed out what he wanted to say in the Chinese text and I used the Latin text to understand him. This was probably one of the best uses yet made of the new Code! As we went on, with great pride and evident joy, he took down from his small supply of books a copy of the documents of the Sec-

ond Vatican Council. It was in Latin. He could not read it.
But he was proud and happy to have it and looked forward
to the day when the documents would be available to him in
Chinese.

I wonder how many American priests or lay Catholics
would proudly show their copy of the Vatican II documents — if they have one. How many, with far less excuse
than this young Chinese priest, would have to admit that they
have never read the documents, at least in their entirety. Or,
like myself, how many would have to admit that they haven't
studied the documents in some years or really made a conscious effort to live them and let their own life be shaped by
what Holy Spirit has had to say to us through the Council.
I am very grateful to the editors of Crossroad for inviting
me to do this volume. It has been for me an enriching and
renewing experience.

It is my hope that the little that has been shared here
will encourage you to go back to the documents themselves
and to let them have an impact upon your life and thinking. Not all the documents have the same value, the same
immediacy, the same practicality. But it sometimes happens,
and it has happened to me, that in the course of reading passages we expect the least from, sudden flashes of insight are
given. Reading all the documents together certainly makes a
powerful impression; they are truly inspiring.

Yes, we do need to go beyond Vatican II. Much has been
happening in these intervening years, in these years that rush
on to the promises and hopes of the twenty-first century.
There has been not only an evolution of human life and society but an important and legitimate development of doctrine
that is essential to the life of the Church that we are.

And, yes, we do need to go back to what was before. The
river of Tradition flows through. It carries to us its essential
and complementary component of the Revelation. It cannot

be cut off at any place without an irreparable loss, a true deformation in the mission of God's People.

But we are all the poorer to the extent to which we have not drawn deeply from the fountains of the Spirit of the Second Vatican Council.

For the past thirty years we have, for the most part, been very busy reforming or seeking to reform the institutions. But how little we have done to renew the vision. What we need so much are true pastors, preachers, and teachers who are *keepers of the vision*. How do we call forth a leadership that is primarily this: keepers of the vision, who help each of us to keep the vision alive and glowing, irradiating all that we do and say and think. Some have argued that we need to return to early Christian practice and let the people elect our leadership, the bishops. Last week an official at the center of one of the mainline churches told me sadly: "We keep electing middle managers." She went on to say that "market logic" was creeping into the Church: "I am no longer a sinner; I'm a customer. The churches are bidding for their share of the market." Without vision we will do no better in electing bishops than those do who appoint them. There is an enormous challenge for us here. How do we prepare people in our culture to recraft institutions so that they truly serve a Spirit-filled, inspiring, and hopeful vision?

I think part of the answer lies in connecting our liturgy, our communal worship, more vitally and intimately with our lives, loves, and work. While up to now it has been in the domain of liturgy that we have done the most in implementing Vatican II, and it is here that the renewal has impacted most directly on the life of the People of God, yet even here it is but a beginning, and for all too many it seems to be largely a matter of only superficial change.

There are among us theologians, leaders, bishops, priests, and laity who are dedicated to elaboration; they are so dedicated to solidifying what is that they hold back the development of the vision. And there are those dedicated to transition; ever moving forward but unable to carry through the vision in any enduring form. We need both. The vision of Vatican II must shine anew, in a new way, for this fourth decade after the Council. And it must be appropriately incarnate in the institutions that we need as a People of God. And it cannot be just a question of balance, albeit a balance very difficult to find and to maintain. Both of these need to be lived to the full: a solidly established vision that is ever evolving to respond to the times and coming to a higher and more effective synthesis if we the Church are going to be able to respond to the aspirations that the Spirit is stirring in the hearts of today's youth and young adults.

I have little doubt that almost everyone who will read this book will be middle-age or older. Many will have their own lived memories of the days of the Council or of the days of change that followed it. But if the tremendous gift the Lord gave us in the Second Vatican Council is going to live on as a vital part of the Tradition, we have to embrace the responsibility of enfleshing this Spirit in our own lives in a credible way and generously and unpossessively passing it on to those who are going to be able to carry it forward into the next century. There is a lot of cynicism abroad. Can the Church really be renewed in the light of an inspiring and hope-giving vision? Or is its whole "renewal" really just a last-ditch effort at self-survival? The vision has to be shiningly clear. And it also has to be clear how the structures of the institution truly serve the incarnation of the vision.

We have to be willing both to live and to die: To live to the full the ever-evolving vision — that vision which is truly illumined now by that great moment of light that was the Second Vatican Council. And to die — to generate and hold the vision dispossessively, willingly passing it on even as it lives in us and enlivens us.

Some speak of ours as a time of discontinuous change. It is so fragmenting, leaving people feeling rootless, unattached, with no sure lifeline, hopeless. It cannot be thus for us. We who believe in the revealing love of God and the Revelation that love has given us know that we do have a life line. But it will guide us, give us surety and hope, only if we keep in touch with it. In daily *lectio,* that vital encounter with the living Spirit in the Word, we need to come into contact with both of the channels of Revelation, the inspired Scriptures and the Tradition — the Tradition that is powerfully expressed for us in the documents of the Second Vatican Council and that needs to be continuously expressed in our lives. It is faithful practice, especially the faithful practice of *lectio* (to use the traditional word for a living encounter with the Lord and his Revelation in and through the written words of Scripture and Tradition) that grounds and enlivens all the other practices, that will enable us peacefully and hopefully, effectively and fruitfully to bridge the discontinuities of our times.

Christ is and remains, as the Council has so powerfully proclaimed, the *Light of the Nations.* He is our Light. In this Light we go forward.

Index